THE HORSE WORLD OF
LONDON

THE FIREMAN'S HORSE

THE
HORSE WORLD OF
LONDON

(1893)

by

W. J. GORDON

A Reprint

DAVID & CHARLES REPRINTS

ISBN 0 7153 5128 1

Originally published in 1893 by
The Religious Tract Society
London

Reprinted in 1971 by
DAVID & CHARLES (PUBLISHERS) LIMITED
South Devon House Newton Abbot
Devon
in conjunction with
J. A. Allen & Company Limited
London SW1

Printed in Great Britain by
Latimer Trend & Company Limited
Whitstable

The Leisure Hour Library.—New Series

THE

HORSE-WORLD OF LONDON

BY

W. J. GORDON

AUTHOR OF

EVERY-DAY LIFE ON THE RAILROAD' 'HOW LONDON LIVES'
'FOUNDRY, FORGE, AND FACTORY' ETC.

LONDON

THE RELIGIOUS TRACT SOCIETY

56 PATERNOSTER ROW AND 65 ST PAUL'S CHURCHYARD

1893

CONTENTS

ILLUSTRATIONS

ROAD CAR COMPANY: HORSES ON FIRST FLOOR, FARM LANE YARD

HORSE-WORLD OF LONDON

CHAPTER I

THE OMNIBUS HORSE

THE omnibuses are the most characteristic feature of
London ; and they increase, while the cabs decrease.
What London would be like without them a recent
strike gave us the opportunity of knowing, and there
can be no doubt that from an æsthetic point of view its
streets would be considerably improved.

But the omnibus is for use, not for beauty ; it exists
for the convenience of the many. It is a money-making
machine, and it looks it, with its crowd of passengers,
who pay up amongst them some forty-four shillings a
day for its hire, as they sit between screens of patchy
advertisements, which add a shilling a day to its
takings, and spoil every attempt at improving its form
and decoration.

We shudder, however, at the thought of depriving
a poor man of his omnibus, and for a writer on horses
to even hint at such a thing is peculiarly ungrateful,
inasmuch as the London General Omnibus Company

are the greatest users of living horse power in London. They have, in round numbers, ten thousand horses, working a thousand omnibuses, travelling twenty million miles in a year, and carrying one hundred and ten million passengers. In other words, every omnibus travels not sixty miles an hour, but sixty miles a day, and every horse travels twelve miles a day. And as an omnibus earns a little over eightpence-halfpenny a mile, and the average fare paid by each passenger is a little under three-halfpence, it follows that each omnibus picks up six passengers every mile.

In practice, a fifth of the omnibuses are daily at rest or under repair, and allowing for these, each vehicle carries thirty-nine passengers during a journey, so that, with its accommodation for twenty-six, three passengers enter and leave for every two of its seats. The average number in an omnibus at any one time is given as fourteen, and averaging these passengers at ten stone apiece, and throwing in the driver and conductor, we get a ton of live weight, to which we can add the ton and a half which the omnibus weighs, making up two-and-a-half tons for the pair to draw, and thus we arrive at the easily-remembered formula that the London omnibus horse draws a ton and a quarter twelve miles a day. He draws this at the rate of five miles an hour ; he is bought when he is five years old ; he works five years; he costs 35*l.* to buy and half-a-sovereign a week to feed ; he is sold for a 5*l.* note ; and lastly, and by no means less importantly, ' he is not a horse, but a mare.'

Most of these mares are English, some of them are Irish, only a few of them are foreign—that is, according

to the dealer, if he can be trusted in his verbal guaran-
tee of nationality. And although the omnibus is of
French extraction, and the London company has a
French offshoot, it is curious that there is so little
avowedly foreign about either the omnibus or its horseflesh. But the omnibus has always been fostered by
the unexpected, even before the public fastened on
' Entreprise générale des omnibus,' and insisted on
giving the vehicle the last word. Who would expect
that Blaise Pascal, the philosopher, was the first
patentee of the omnibus ? It seems more incongruous
than that the hansom should have been first patented
by the architect of Birmingham Town Hall and of
Arundel Roman Catholic chapel. Who would have expected that any new vehicle for the living would be
introduced by an undertaker ? And yet it was Shillibeer ' de Paris,' the funeral performer, who brought
over the omnibus in 1829 : a three-horse affair, with
twenty-two inside passengers and a library of books to
amuse them—a library of ' standard authors which no
omnibus should be without.' Twenty years afterwards
the Shillibeer 'bus developed unexpectedly into the small
' twelve inside and two out' variety ; in 1857 it sud-
denly sported the ' knife-board ' ; and thirty years after
that it began to bear the ' garden-seat ' which Captain
Molesworth invented, which the Road Car Company introduced, and with which the two vehicles a week turned
out at Highbury by the 'London General' are all fitted—
which vehicles, by the way, cost 5*l.* a cwt. to build.

But it is not with the vehicles, but with the horses
that we are concerned. Let us be off to some typical

yard to see how these horses live and how they are cared for ; and let the yard be one of the newest, say, that at Chelverton Road.   Here are the 375 horses working the 'white 'bus' line from Putney to Liverpool Street. The white 'buses are well known for their trimness.   Their colour precludes their being carelessly looked after, but they are no better kept than the others.   Like the rest, they are cleaned and overhauled every morning, their locks looked to, their tires examined, their wheels tapped, just as if they were railway carriages, the minor repairs being done on the spot, the more serious being executed at Highbury.

Each of these omnibuses has its driver, its conductor, and its ' stud ' of ten or eleven horses, the eleven being required when the vehicle does its four full trips and a short one in a day.   The full trip averages three hours and a half, and the day's work thus employs eight horses, giving each pair in turn a day's rest, but the extra short trip means an extra horse and a different system of relief, which we can deal with later on.

The horses are of all colours, bay, roan, brown, chestnut, grey, and that most promising of all colours, flea-bitten grey, which is seldom worn by a bad horse. All over the country, at the fairs and the provincial stables, buyers are at work for the company, picking out the peculiar class of horse which will best bear the constant stopping and starting of the London omnibus traffic.   When an omnibus is full it weighs three and a quarter tons, a considerable weight for a pair to start.   Think of it, ye exigent women, who rather than walk a yard will stop an omnibus twice in a minute ;

the sudden stopping and starting, so often unnecessary, taking more out of a horse than an hour's steady tramp on the level, and being the chief cause of the London horse's poor expectation of life.

When the horses are bought they are sent to the depôt at Paddington or to that at Spitalfields, where they are sorted out for the different roads. Five years on the London streets takes as much out of a horse as ten years elsewhere; and a horse that will suit one road will not suit another, owing to the different kinds of paving. There is one road worked over by one of the ' Favourite' lines on which there is no asphalt; there are others which have every variety of material, the worst being asphalt when slightly wet, the best being wood when lightly sprinkled with gravel. But it is not so much the paving as the change from one sort to another which is so puzzling to the horses, the sudden break from granite to asphalt, cr macadam to wood, requiring an instant change in the step, to which not every horse is equal, though by some the knack is caught in a week or so.

The new horse is sent off to the yard from which the road he has been chosen for is worked. This is the headquarters from which the omnibus begins its travels in the morning, and to which it returns at night after its four or five journeys to and fro. The 'Putneys,' for example, start eastwards to Liverpool Street, and their last journey is a westerly one; the Walham Green ' Favourites ' work northwards to Islington and back; the Victoria 'Favourites' work southwards from Holloway and back; the 'Royal Blues' from Victoria, northwards and back; and so with all the rest, always out

LONDON GENERAL OMNIBUS COMPANY'S HORSES

and home, though on some lines the horses are not changed at the yard, but at some corner close by.

The new-comer is exercised in a two-horse brake, and as soon as found fit is placed alongside its future companion. Each stable contains as a rule two studs, one on the right-hand, one on the left, each row with two gaps together for the pair out at work. Every horse is branded on the hoof; and on the wall over each head is a plate giving the number of the horse, the colour, and the date of purchase. Some of the young ones will be worked out in eighteen months, some will last seven years; but the same pair are worked together till one of them fails, and in the eleven-horse studs it is the one odd horse which is changed about. Each horse has its own collar, which hangs near the number-plate, for horse collars are made in sizes like men's collars, and no good work can be done if the collar is ill-fitting.

As a rule the horses look better in the stable than they do in harness, and their home is neater than might be supposed : the eight or nine of them in a row on each side standing in peat, for there is no straw; the plates and collars in a line above their heads; the long sliding skylights aloft; the brick floor with the clean-swept gangway, having the door at one end and the bin at the other.

The unit of organisation is the stud, and every stud is in charge of a horsekeeper, against whom is charged the forage and other bills, just as the coal and oil bills are charged against an engine-driver on a railroad. The provender for 10,000 horses runs into large figures during a year. The chief item is maize, of which 115,000 quarters, or 25,000 tons, are eaten; of oats 8,000 quarters, or 1,075 tons, are run through; of beans and peas 12,300 quarters, or 2,700 tons—making up 29,000 tons of grain, in addition to 8,000 quarters of bran and 20,000 loads of hay and straw and mixture— a pretty little forage bill, working out, as we have said, at almost ten shillings a week per horse.

Even the shoeing costs 20,000*l.* a year, averaging a shoe a week for each horse, and including frost nails in cold weather—poor weak things for such rough work, which, as a rule, are worn down long before the commencement of the return journey. Should a horse fall, it is the driver's duty to get it up again; but should it be badly injured, it is the conductor's duty to go to the nearest telegraph station, wire to the yard, and remain by the horse till the cart comes; while the driver, looking the most miserable of men, takes home the vehicle with the remaining horse.

Two out of every three horses die in the service, and the carcases sold have exceeded 1,300 in the year. Only such horses as are likely to thoroughly recover are taken care of, the 'bad lives' being remorselessly weeded out. But though the horse is, of course, looked upon as a machine—for sentiment pays no dividend—there is a pleasant friendship between horse and man which not everyone would suspect.

It was a novel experience being driven from yard to yard by one of the foremen in his gig. He had charge of about a thousand horses, and almost everyone he knew by sight, and could tell the stud it belonged to and the stable and place in which it stood; and he was, apparently, posted up in the history of every horse in every omnibus we met.

'See that nice little mare on the near side? A month ago she had paralysis in her back, but we pulled her through, we did. There comes another, the off one; she has been having a bad sore throat, poor thing,

THE INVALID: WASHING THE WOUND

but she's better, good old soul!' And a moment later: 'Here's a pair of big 'uns. The grey trod on a French nail, and a nice job we had to get the foot right. The near 'un had fever in the feet very bad last month; that isn't so serious: it is a very common complaint. Oh! you brute!'—this to a showy-looking bay in another omnibus. 'I wish you no harm though! Of all the tempers that ever spoilt a good horse you've got the worst. That's the lion and the lamb, I call them. The lamb had congestion of the lungs a little while ago. I found her very bad one Sunday morning, and thought we were going to lose her, but no! and there she is as tough as nails.' And with a lift of the whip elbow, answered by a similar lift on the part of the omnibus driver, we exchange the usual salute as we pass by. And when we reach the next yard we hear our friend ordering a pint and a half of ale for one horse, mustard for another, a blister for another, poultices for two or three, and 'a drop of whisky for the roan at the far end,' while there is a general feeling of sympathy all round.

The veterinary bill is 3,000*l.* a year, the work being contracted for by local 'vets' in the different districts, each of whom has charge of so many yards. The ordinary ailments—most of them curiously human—are dealt with at the yards, and when extra care is required the patients are sent to the infirmary at the headquarters of the district; but this happens to few, and practically the horse passes all its life in the streets and stables. Once upon a time the company put its horses out to grass at Woodford, but that practice has been given up.

The London General owns nearly half the omnibuses in London, and is the largest concern of the kind in the world. Next to it in London comes the Road Car Company, which carries 37,000,000 passengers a year, and has about 300 cars and 3,000 horses. The company has been running about ten years, and is favourably known as the introducer of the garden seat and the pioneer of the penny fares and the roll tickets. It is worked on much the same system as the London General, but being a younger company has fewer survivals.

At Farm Lane, Fulham, the Road Car Company has the finest omnibus yard in Britain. At half-past seven in the morning when the first car comes out, and indeed at any time, it is one of the sights of London. In the central court are over sixty cars which have been washed and examined during the night, the cleaning of each seven being one man's night's work. Around the quadrangle are the stables, on two storeys, and in them are 700 horses. Four of the floors have each about fourteen studs of eleven in a long double line standing in peat, the gas jets down the middle alight in the fading darkness flickering on the double set of harness for each stud, which gleams black and shiny on the posts that make the long lines look longer, while the growing daylight streams in from the high windows on the inner wall and from the ventilators overhead.

There is a strong Caledonian element in the ' Road Car,' and even the horses are most of them Scotch. Like those of the ' General ' they cost about 35*l*. each, begin work when about five years old, last about five years, and fetch about thirty shillings each as carcases for the cat's-meat man. When they first come into the stable they are put to light work with an experienced companion, and it is on an average eight weeks before they get into full working order. The studs are all elevens, the car doing five full trips a day. The eleven, with the one horse working round as a relief, means one horse resting every day, and Sunday being a short day,

ROAD CAR COMPANY : FARM LANE YARD

with a trip the less, affords a chance of a rest for three
horses every seventh day.

The day's work of an omnibus horse is, in fact,
severe but short, and he spends at least five-sixths of his
time in the stable, making friends with his neighbours,
or trying to get the better of them, for there are many
points of resemblance other than pathological between
equine and human nature. And surely a little touchi-
ness can be forgiven after a worrying trip through
noisy London in rain or snow or fog, varied at all sorts
of irregular intervals with sudden stops and starts on
greasy asphalt; the start, as we said before, being for
a full load a pull of between three and four tons.

A road car of the latest type is said to weigh a ton
and a half; as a matter of fact it weighs thirty-three
hundredweight, and it costs, lettering and all, 160*l.*
Adjoining the Farm Lane yard the Car Company have
their building works, and here the car can be seen
'from its birth to its grave,' a stage carriage in all
stages, including its helpless condition during its week
of repair. For once a year each car comes into shop
to be dismantled and overhauled, when all its working
parts, and even its springs, are taken to pieces, and
condemned if unsound.

In these shops is an interesting set of wheel-making
machinery—a nave machine, that with its cutters at
different lengths and of different widths, shapes a nave
at one operation; a radial machine, that shapes the
fellies, the mystic seven of which form the ring that
takes the twice seven spokes; a trueing machine that
finishes the woodwork; and a tiring table—not of the
Queen Anne type—that rises from a well to hold the

wheel and the glowing tire, and sinks back into the
water with a hiss and a seethe as the hot iron cools and
grips itself into place.   The wheels of a car are a
means of its identification.   By the colour of the body
you tell the line the vehicle travels ; by the colour of
the wheels you tell the company to which it belongs.

Besides the 'General' and the 'Road Cars,' there
are the Omnibus Carriage Company, the Railway omnibuses, including the Metropolitan, now lighted by oil
gas or electricity ; the omnibuses owned by the Tramway Companies, the Camden Town, and Star, and other
associations, and the private owners, ranging down to
that fortunately rare 'unfairest of the fare,' the man
with one vehicle, the so-called 'pirate' or 'flat-catcher,'
who cruises as he likes and charges what he pleases ;
an irregular man who makes up for the erasures in his
fare-table by an exuberance of expletives—at least,
as a rule, though there are in London some of the
honestest and mildest-mannered pirates imaginable,
with the very neatest and completest of turn-outs.

Every omnibus or road car allowed to ply in London
has to be approved of and licensed by the Scotland
Yard authorities.   About five per cent. are refused a
licence every year, and thus weeded out by the police,
for being too old or unsafe to pass muster—some of
them condemned in the daylight at the annual examination, some of them discovered and doomed in the
night time at the monthly inspection.   The annual
police return gives the present number of licensed
omnibuses at 2,210, but this does not include the
trams, of which we shall have something to say by-and-
by.   These 2,210 vehicles we can assume to require

ROAD CAR HORSES

22,000 horses and 11,000 men to look after them and their burden. The horses, at something under 35*l.* each, would represent three quarters of a million of money, and the stables and buildings they occupy are worth at least another quarter of a million, for those of the London General and the Road Car are valued at 200,000*l.* The million is thus made up by the 'bus horse and his home, and his food costs over 10,000*l.* a week ; the 2,200 odd vehicles average 150*l.* apiece to build, which means a third of a million for the lot ; and if we add to this a sixth of a million for the value of the harness and the stores generally, after making all allowance for depreciation on every point, we shall make up another half million, and, adding our figures together, be well within the limit in estimating that it takes fifteen hundred thousand pounds to work the omnibus trade of London.

The tram came into existence to save the horse, it being shown clearly enough that the introduction of the rail meant the reduction of resistance and the easing of the horse's work; but, as a company for merely lightening a horse's labour would hardly be floatable, it was at once proposed to increase the weight and carrying capacity of the vehicle, so that the investor might share advantages with the horse. As a consequence, the poor horse is 20 per cent. worse off now than he was before the invention of the rail.

The average working life of a London omnibus horse is five years; that of a tram horse is only four. He is the same sort of horse; he comes to work at the same age; he costs about the same ; and he works the same few hours ; but so much greater is his effort that it costs a shilling a week more to feed him, and he is worked out in four-fifths of the time.

From the horse's point of view tramming, as we now have it, is by no means the perfect system of loco-motion that some people imagine. In the testing-room there may be but a trifling difference between the resistance experienced by a wheel on a raised rail, and that of one on a sunk rail ; but this difference becomes enormous in practice, particularly in a climate and on a soil such as London's. The railway rail stands up clear and clean ; the tramway rail is generally clogged with dirt, besides being burdened with the additional friction caused by the flange of the wheel. As an object lesson in this matter take a railway horse engaged in shunting ; watch the ease with which it starts and the weight it draws, as shown even by the tare of the trucks, and compare it with the effort made by a tram horse. It is a fact that the amount of resistance on a dirty tram-rail is almost as much as that on wood pavement, and if all the London roads were of wood the lives of a tram horse and a 'bus horse would be in the inverse ratio of the weights of their vehicles.

A two-horse car weighs two and three quarter tons when empty, and double this when full, which is a good weight for horses in daily work, particularly when it is remembered that a gradient of 1 in 100 doubles it, while 1 in 50 trebles it ; and that although the tractive force is about a hundredth of the load on the level, yet four or five times the pull is needed to start a car as will keep it going—and a car averages 500 separate starts a day. A slope of 1 in 50 is not particularly

steep; it is, in fact, the prevailing gradient of the
London Tramways Company, while that of the North
Metropolitan up to the Angel is 1 in 40. The gradients are of course the same for the omnibuses as for the
trams, but it does not require much of a mathematician
to discover that there is a great difference between the
doubling and trebling of $3\frac{1}{2}$ and the doubling and
trebling of $5\frac{1}{2}$.

There are just under 10,000 tram horses in London,
most of them working two-horse cars; these cars being
generally worked with a stud of eleven horses, in the
same way as the horses of the London Road Car Company
already described, each pair doing but one trip averaging
thirteen miles a day out and home, the car travelling
65 miles, and picking up on its journeys about nine
passengers per mile.

London has 135 miles of tram line, of which 88 are
double, and over these 135 miles the thousand cars,
less the percentage under repair, accomplish a mileage
of 21,000,000 miles in a year and carry 190,000,000
passengers. These 190,000,000 passengers pay a
million of money in fares, so that 190 are carried for
a sovereign, and the average amount paid by each
person for each ride is a penny farthing.

The greatest number of horses are owned by the
North Metropolitan Company, who have nearly 3,500,
being the largest number owned in the kingdom by any
one tram company or municipality; the London Tramways Company have about 150 less. These are the
two chief companies, and between them they possess
two-thirds of the horse-power. Next to them comes the
London Street Tramways Company, with about 1,200

THE NEXT CHANGE

horses, the South London filling fourth place with
about 800.   London has more tramways than any other
place; there are 13 companies in it altogether, and
these companies own half the tram horses of England,
and their horses mount up in value to nearly a third of
a million sterling.

On June 30, 1890, the capital paid up by these
companies was 3,561,000*l.*   Adding to this what we
arrived at for the omnibus trade, we obtain the mystic
5,000,000*l.*, which enables us to say with a fair approach
to accuracy that to work the London trams and omnibuses one pound has had to be invested for every
member of London's population.

CHAPTER II

THE CAB HORSE

IT would at first sight seem to be an easy task to arrive at the number of London cab horses.

Every cab has to be licensed, and the number of licences is given annually in the Metropolitan Police Commissioner's Report. A year or so ago 11,297 were granted in the London district, and as there are two horses to a cab in proper working we have only to double the 11,297 to obtain the horse power; and further, as a cab horse is worth 30*l*., we have only to multiply by that amount to get—an exaggerated notion of the facts of the case.

The genus 'cab' comprises two species, the 'hansom' and the 'clarence,' the first having two wheels, the other four; but these species are divisible into several varieties, especially the clarence, which varies from the not particularly sumptuous down to the positively disgraceful. As it is with the vehicles, so it is with the horses, and so it is with the men.

It is in the night-time that we find the lowest grade of horse, cab, and man; but as these are seen by the few we may look to the next variety in the scale. This is the Sunday cab, particularly the sort

THE NIGHT CAB

that appears in the morning. Last Sunday we had a typical specimen at the corner of our street. The cab was hired from one man, the harness from another, the horse from another. And there are cabs in London on a Sunday in which even the driver's badge has been hired, although, of course, this is illegal.

The horse was a cab horse for the day. On the Monday morning he would be in the shafts of a coal-cart dragging 'prime Wallsend' at a shilling a hundredweight; and in front of the Wallsend he would spend the week till Saturday night, when he would again be hired out and turn his attention from coals to cabs. The cab itself is at night work all the week; of the many animals that draw it there is not one that has not toiled in some other trade during some hours of the day; and so far from its having two horses it never really has one. In fact, we have here a variety of cab horse that is not a cab horse at all.

Cab horses can be conveniently classified in a series of sevenths, according to the number of days of the week they spend in the cab shafts. There are some that go cabbing one day a week, some two, some three, some four, some five, some six. The six-day variety is the genuine article; he does nothing but draw cabs, for no true cab horses—or, at least, but a very, very few—work seven days a week. He is the commonest horse; next to him coming the four-seventh animal. This horse appears in a cab on Sundays, Tuesdays, Wednesdays, and Thursdays only; on Friday he is engaged in taking home the washing, that is his easiest day's work; on Saturday he is very much more engaged in taking home washing; and on Monday he has his hardest day in collecting the washing it takes him two days to deliver. Another variety is the three-sevenths horse, who, as a rule, appears in a cab on Sundays, Wednesdays, and Thursdays, and works miscellaneously during the other four days. All these odd fractional horses come out on Sunday, when the regular cab horse is at rest. There are, however, some regular cab horses doing Sunday work, and these have their day's rest generally on Tuesday.

Of the 11,297 licensed cabs 917 were reported during the year as unfit for use, and we may take them from the total; we may also remove a proportion of the night cabs worked under the curious conditions already alluded to, and the really good cabs under repair, and for other considerations make other deductions, until we find that London on any one day had never more than 9,000 workable cabs. Of these, about two out of three have the two horses, the rest averaging hardly a horse apiece. This gives us 15,000 horses at the outside, and averaging these at 30*l.* we find that they are worth 450,000*l.*

Curiously enough, there were in the year 15,336 licensed cab-drivers, so that there was practically a horse for every man, the surplus of men over cabs being easily accounted for by the fact that the percentage of cabs at work is greater than the percentage of men. Of the 15,000 men about 14 per cent. were convicted during the year for offences ranging from cruelty to drunkenness, in addition to those convicted of the minor offences of loitering and obstruction ; and including most of these there was a large per-

centage appearing on the masters' books as having proved
themselves untrustworthy. Clearing away this regret-
table fringe, we should be left with a little more than a
cab a man.

The London cab trade is at a standstill, or rather
it is declining. During the last three years the
London trams have increased at the rate of $8\frac{1}{2}$ per cent.,
while the omnibuses have increased at the rate of
17 per cent. Instead of increasing, the cabs have
decreased. In 1888—when the London hackney
carriage list stood higher than it has ever done since
Captain Bailey, fresh from Raleigh's Guiana expedition,
started the first four carriages at London's first cab-
stand, the Maypole in the Strand—there were 7,396
hansoms and 4,013 four-wheelers; there are now
7,376 hansoms and 8,921 four-wheelers.

This state of affairs is due in some measure to the
cost of cab-riding as compared with that of other means
of locomotion; but it is due in a greater degree to the
uncertainty that exists regarding the fare that will
satisfy the cabman. It is not the sixpence a mile that
people object to, or even a shilling a mile, but the 'living
margin'; and so long as a cabman has to depend
more or less on charity—for that is what the voluntary
addition to his fare amounts to—so long will the crowd
flock to railway, tramway, omnibus, and railway omnibus, in which they know exactly what they have to pay,
and can pay it without injuring any delicate suscepti-
bilities. The pressure on the cabman is, however,
great; he is rarely his own master; he has to pay the
owner so much a day for the hire of the horse and

C

cab, and he has to make what he can out of the public, the owner varying the cost of hire in accordance with the man's opportunities, the idea being that the capitalist should make his profit in the summer and give the worker a share in it. But this plan of trusting to squeezability is not a success. While the cab-list diminishes there is an increase in both wings of the opposition, not only in the omnibuses and cars of the commonalty, but in the livery broughams and private carriages, whose hirers and owners are the cabmen's best friends. And consequently the only horses in London that do not increase are the cab horses.

Our cab horses are generally Irish, many of them being shipped from Waterford. They come over unshod, in order that they may do no damage, and to keep them quiet they have their lips tied down; and what with this lip-tying, and the sea passage, and the change of climate, it takes them about eight weeks to get into working order, during which they are gradually drilled into shape, first in double harness and then in single harness, round the squares and quiet thoroughfares.

As a rule, they are four years old when they arrive, they cost 30*l*., they last only three years, and they are then sold for 9*l*. to go into the tradesman's cart; but horses are rising in value, and cost more to buy and fetch more to sell than they used to do. This, of course, refers to the bulk of the horses, which, as in the omnibus service, are mostly mares. There are some that cost more, some that cost less; some that last longer, some that do not last as long; and on the cab-rank there is a fair sprinkling of British horses and a few foreigners, but the thoroughbreds of whom we have heard are as rare as the doctors, warriors, and members of the Athenæum Club who are said to drive them.

A cab horse is well fed ; hansom horses average a sack of corn each a week ; and they want it, for in the six days during the season they are driven over two hundred miles. There is nothing out of the way in a day's work of forty miles ; and this with a weight of half a ton behind, including the cab and driver, but not the passengers. The way in which the horse is worked varies in different yards and with different men. There are over 3,500 cab-owners in London, and as some of them own a hundred and more cabs, there must be a large number who have but one or two cabs, and perhaps two or three horses, when the horses have a hard time of it. Many are worked on the ' one horse power' principle, in which the cab, generally a four-wheeler, goes out at eight in the morning and comes back at eight at night. The four-wheelers that frequent the railway stations have two horses, the first going out at seven in the morning and returning about two in the afternoon, the second going out to stay at the station till ten, and then perhaps loitering about the theatres with a view to picking up a last fare. This participation of the railway cab in theatre work is a sore point with the ordinary cabman, who has not the entry to the railway platforms. One company there is with an express due in a little before eleven for which the cabs have to wait, and greatly would it please the unprivileged cabmen of our streets

if the other companies would each bring in a late
express under similar conditions.

There are some cabs ' double tide working,' going
out at eight o'clock in the morning, returning at seven
at night, and going out again immediately with another
horse and man and not returning till six next morning,
when, after two hours for cleaning up, they are off
again on their day-journey.   In the ' long day working '
usual among the larger masters the cab goes out at
nine o'clock, returns between three and five for a fresh
horse, and comes home at midnight; while some are at
work from noon till two o'clock next morning; but in
these larger yards the invariable rule is that both horse
and man have one day's rest in seven.

When a horse is bought by the cab-master it is
occasionally numbered, but oftener named from some
trivial circumstance connected with its purchase, or
from some event chronicled in the morning newspapers.
A whole chapter might be written on the names of the
London cab horses, which are assuredly more curious
than elegant.   Three horses we know of bought on a
hot day were Scorch, Blaze, and Blister ; three others
bought on a dirty morning were Mud, Slush, and
Puddle ; two brought home in a snowstorm were
named Sleet and Blizzard ; four that came in the rain
were Oilskin, Sou'-wester, Gaiters, and Umbrella.
Even the time of day has furnished a name, and Ten-
o'clock, Eight-sharp, and Nine-fifteen have been met
with, though perhaps Two-two owed more to the
æsthete than the horologer.   Some horses are named
from the peculiarities of the dealer or his man, and in

one stable there were at one time Curseman, Sandy-
man, Collars, Necktie, Checkshirt, and Scarfpin. The
political element is, of course, manifest, and in almost
every stable there are Roseberies and Randies, Salis-
buries and Gladstones, Smiths and Dizzies. Some
stables are all Derby winners, some all dramas, some
all songs, some all towns. It is the exception for a
horse to be named after any peculiarity of its own,
unless it be an objectionable one; and it would never
do to give it a Christian name, with or without a
qualifying adjective, which might lead to its being
mistaken for one of the men in the yard.

The favourite colour for a cab horse is brown; the
one least sought after is grey. A grey horse will not
do in a hansom, unless for railway work where the cabs
are taken in rotation and the quality or colour of the
horse is of no consequence. Why clubland should
object to grey horses is not known, but the fact remains
that a man with a grey horse will get fewer fares with
him than with a brown one. One explanation is that
the light hairs float off and show on dark clothes, but
this is hardly satisfying, and it seems safer to put the
matter down to fashion. Anyhow, a hansom cabman
will not take out a grey horse if he can help it, unless
it be an exceptionally 'gassy' one, gassy being 'cab-
bish' for showy. But not so a four-wheeler man; if
he can have a grey horse he will, the reason being that
if ever a housemaid goes for a cab she will, if she has a
choice, pick out the grey horse. At least, so says the
trade, which may, of course, be prejudiced or roman-
cing; but the prejudice or the romance is known all
over London. The curious chance may be owing to the

THE HANSOM HORSE AND ITS DRIVER

proverb that ' the grey mare is the better horse,' which, like many other proverbs, is merely an allusion gone wrong.

Some horses, like these ' gassy ' greys, begin their cab-life in a hansom and end it in a four-wheeler; but this is not done by the large masters, who keep their horses distinct, and clear them out to Rymill's or Aldridge's for dispersal. Some masters drive their own cabs, and naturally take good care of their own property ; but with the bulk of the cabmen the horse is a machine, hired out as one might hire out a tricycle, and returned in a sufficiently sound state to avoid comment. The man finds the horse and cab ready for him in the morning ; he leaves his licence as security for his return ; and he drives off in search of fares. When he comes back he simply hands the cab over as it stands, pays up—or not—at the office, and hurries out of the yard. Some there are who will look over the horse before he is put into the shafts, and follow him into the stable on their return, and treat him more as a friend ; but there are not many of these when we come to percentages. But as a horse that suits one man will not suit another—for horses differ as well as the men—it is usual to give the old hands the same horses every day. It is curious how dependent the cabman is on his horse; every day horses will come back with whom, according to the cabman's account, ' it is impossible to earn any money,' and next day these horses will be taken out by other men who will be loud in their praise, and drive them for months afterwards until the day comes when they are returned with contempt and the man will demand a fresh horse ' to

THE CAB STAND: ON THE RANK

change his luck,' much as a card-player will take a fresh chair.

London has 600 cabstands, exclusive of those in the City and on private ground, such as the railway stations. A few of these are always full ; a few have never had a cab on them even though they may have existed for years. The 600 cabstands on an average afford accommodation for eleven vehicles each. The rest of the cabs are either carrying passengers or else plying empty along such streets as Piccadilly, where they are a nuisance to all but those who want cabs. The same thing may, however, be said of the cabstands, and, considering the convenience that 'crawlers' afford, it is only the very strenuous reformer who would abolish them entirely, if it were possible to do so.

Out of the 15,000 cabmen, about 2,000 are convicted every year for drunkenness, cruelty, wilful misbehaviour, loitering, plying, obstruction, stopping on the wrong side of the road, delaying, leaving their cabs unattended, &c., &c. The cabman who 'knows his business best' is the one who can crawl judiciously without getting into trouble with the police, resulting for a first offence in the famous 'two-and-six and two,' which means half-a crown fine and a florin costs.

At many of the stands there is a ' shelter,' which is much larger inside than a glance at the exterior would lead one to suppose. The shelters are generally farmed from the Shelter Fund Society by some old cabman. They are the cabman's restaurants, and the cabman, as a rule, is not so much a large drinker as a large eater.

At one shelter lately the great feature was boiled rabbit and pickled pork at two o'clock in the morning, and for weeks a small warren of Ostenders was consumed nightly.

The two-wheeler improves every year. There are many hansoms now in London as good in every way as private carriages, and these will often have a fifty-guinea horse in their shafts. The four-wheeler improves but microscopically, and, though it becomes no worse than it used to be, it touches a depth which is by no means desirable. Most cabs are varnished twice a year, some are varnished but once, and that, of course, is just before inspection day, when the new annual licence is applied for. On that morning many a newly-varnished mockery will journey gingerly to Clerkenwell, and just satisfy the inspector's lenient eye, returning triumphantly with the inside and outside plates and the stencilled certificate on its back, which show that the vehicle has passed muster, and that the owner has paid 2*l.* for a licence to work it in the London streets. Besides the 2*l.*, the owner has to pay fifteen shillings carriage duty to Somerset House; and, for a licence and the badge to drive, the cabman has to pay to the police five shillings.

The cabman has to pass an examination as well as the vehicle, but the vehicle is examined every year, while the cabman is only examined once, and then not in personal appearance, though there may be a bias that way, but in an elementary knowledge of London topography. The knowledge required is not very great, and 1,500 candidates apply in a year, but it is interesting to note that out of every 100 candidates 34 are

THE GROWLER: HORSE AND MAN

' ploughed '—a much higher percentage of rejections than exists among the vehicles.

The cabman takes his licence to the owner whom he desires to make his ' master.' He takes the cab out on trust, leaving his licence as a deposit so long as he remains in the same employment. The engagement is terminable at any time, and when the man changes masters his old master has to fill in on the back of his licence the length of time he has been in his service. At the end of the year the man takes the endorsed licence accounting for his year's work to New Scotland Yard, and there gets a clean one covering another twelve months.

The amount paid by the man for the day's hire varies with the vehicle, the master, and the season. It is much less really than it is nominally, owing to the numerous occasions on which allowances are made for bad luck and bad weather. Continuous wet is not cabmen's weather; what they like is a showery day, or, what is better, a fine morning and a wet afternoon, or a series of scorching hot days when people find the other means of conveyance too stuffy for comfort. Although the amount is frequently stated to be more, the average for hansoms during the last year over several yards was nine shillings for the first three months in the year, then a rise every week of a shilling a day to the end of May, when it remained at the maximum of eighteen shillings till the second week in June, when it dropped a shilling a week down to the nine shillings at which it will remain for the rest of the year. The height of the London cab season is thus from the Derby week to the Ascot week, the one day being the Thurs-

day after the Derby. If you wish to go to the Derby
in a hansom you pay 3*l.*, of which 1*l.* is extra profit, it
being estimated that the man would have taken 2*l.* if
he remained in London. And, curiously enough, the
distance to and from Epsom is the average day's journey
of a London cab horse.

The weight he draws is in inverse ratio to his
strength. The hansom weighs from eight to ten
hundredweight; the newer ones weigh about nine
hundredweight and a half, and cost a hundred guineas;
the four-wheeler does not cost as much, and is heavier.
The hansoms carry three persons, including the driver,
the four-wheelers take six, besides the luggage; and
yet the hansom horse is, if anything, the stronger of
the two. In general work the hansom has but one
passenger, the four-wheeler rarely less than two; and
altogether the clarence horse has much the worst time
of it. The cabs are licensed to carry so many passengers,
but there is no limit to the weight of the luggage,
and it seems nobody's business to keep down the
load, which, for the light class of horse used, is often
great.

The packing of four-wheelers, particularly at low-
class weddings and funerals, is occasionally alarming.
Passing through Wandsworth not long ago, the writer
saw a miserably weedy bay mare toiling up the East
Hill with a four-wheeler in which was a wedding-party
of five ample people inside, a 16-stone woman on the
box, three large men on the roof, and three hobble-
dehoys behind; and this up a long gradient of 1 in
25 which the tram company dare not attempt, preferring
to leave a gap in their system between the bottom and

top of it. Luckily a wedding-party such as this does not come often and does not last long, but it deserves mention as one of the unpleasant experiences of a cab horse's life.

The every-day cab horse lives in a mews, a row of stables on a ground floor opening out on to a long courtyard roughly paved with that pitching which lets gallons of wet and slush soak between it, so that many of the stones rest on a film of black mud that squeezes up at every shower. Were it not for the embarrassing fact that a fragrant mews is invariably healthy, the sanitary authorities would probably have insisted before this on the paving of these stable-yards being much more closely laid. In many cases much of the drainage is between the stones into the earth, and not into dry earth, but into clayey ground saturated with washings of hundreds of horses. A prominent object in these yards, the stones of which are clean enough on the surface, is the manure heap, which, so far from being a source of income, has now to be paid for to be taken away. All over London horse owners are growling about this manure question. At one time the manure was worth threepence a horse a week; happy is the man who can nowadays get a farthing a week per horse for it; many give it away, and there are a large number who are obliged to pay for its removal as trade refuse. Most of the stables have been converted for cab purposes, but some have been specially built, and there are one or two yards in which the stables are in storeys and the horses are upstairs on the second and third floors.

Some cab-stables are very disorderly; some, whether

with straw or peat litter, are quite patterns of neatness On a Sunday morning most of the London cab horses are at home. Quiet as they might be in the shafts, they are a restless lot when together, and after the inevitable Saturday pail of bran mash, it is a common practice to give them their Sunday provender uncut, in order to keep them quiet by giving them something to do. They are as a rule fed well, so as to get the maximum of work out of them during their short career; although there is, of course, a limit beyond which food is wasted so far as efficiency is concerned. Some of the horses find their work too much for them before a year is out; some last five or six years; some spend the year round at work; some are turned out to grass for a couple of months.

If the cab horse could choose his track he would have neither asphalt nor granite blocks; good macadam is good enough for him, though wood is better, if very wet or very dry and not quite bare of gravel. Like all town horses he comes oftenest to grief where the roadway changes, and he suffers from much the same ailments as the omnibus horse, with a rather greater partiality for picking up nails. When he dies in the shafts he is worth as many shillings as he cost pounds; but, as we have hinted, he usually retires from the trade fractionally, and makes his last appearance as a fare-earner in that shabbiest of all vehicles, the London Sunday morning cab.

Bulking the London cabs together, we can estimate the turn-out complete, cab, horse, and harness, at 100*l.* ; and 9,000 of these mean 900,000*l.* The 6,000 additional horses at 30*l.* each yield 180,000*l.* The stable accommodation, freehold and leasehold, the fittings and sundries, and plant and working cash, would certainly be cheaply bought for 170,000*l*., and that gives us a million and a quarter to work the London cab trade, which is surely quite enough.

CHAPTER III

THE CARRIER'S HORSE

THE carrying trade of these days is in the hands of the railway companies, and the carrier's horse is for all practical purposes the railway horse. Of the 84,000,000 tons of general merchandise hauled along the railroads of this island in 1890, the bulk was collected and distributed in railway vans.

A railway company is obliged to keep several varieties of horse in its stables. It must have horses that walk for the heavy traffic, and horses that trot for the light; or, to put it differently, waggon horses, goods horses, parcels horses, horses for shunting, and horses for omnibuses in the cases in which its omnibuses are not horsed by contract. And, taking all these varieties together, we find that the companies collecting and delivering goods in the metropolis have amongst them a stud of 6,000. These we shall not be over-valuing at 60*l.* apiece all round, which means that railway shareholders have some 360,000*l.* invested in horseflesh in London' alone, to say nothing of the vans and drays, which would be worth quite as much.

The typical railway horse is the van horse, of which ten-thirteenths of the stud consist. He is not specially

D

bred for his calling; he is but a dray horse whom the association of certain merits has peculiarly fitted for railway work. There is no mistaking this horse; he is a Britisher to the backbone, but he is not so easy to get as he used to be, owing to the foreigners collecting so many specimens of him. He is as good a horse as we have, being power personified, with nothing about him in wasteful excess. Well-moulded in every muscle, standing not an inch too high on his well-shaped legs —' give me legs and feet,' said the Midland superintendent to us, ' and I will look after the rest,'—broad and strong, with nothing of tubbiness in the barrel or scragginess about the neck and head, he is admirably adapted for the work for which he is chosen; and that work he does well.

In these days, when a corn-chandler will forage your horse at threepence an inch of height a week—so many hands so many shillings—it is the inches of bulk that give a van horse his value, and some of the heavier horses in the four-horse teams will weigh nineteen hundredweight and be worth a hundred guineas, while the average horse working in a pair will weigh two hundredweight or so less, and cost proportionately less to buy, though very little less to keep.

The Great Western prides itself on having as good a stud as any company in London, and the stables in which it is housed are admittedly excellent. In the new block in South Wharf Road there are four floors of horses one over the other, the top floor being almost as high as the hotel, with a look-out down on to the station roof. Sunday is the railway horse's day of rest, a day which all of them know, though they may not call it by

A MOVING MASS OF THIRTEEN TONS

that name, and for seeing the horse at home, quiet and contented, under exceptionally favourable circumstances, there is no place better than Paddington. In the new stables there are about 500 horses; close by, nearer the goods station, there is another lot of 140, comfortably installed under lofty arches, which are sensibly ventilated and lighted electrically ; and further on there is the infirmary, with three dozen stables for invalids. Altogether, the Great Western has about 1,100 horses working in London, the largest outlying detachment being in Goswell Road, just on the City boundary, where 200 answer the needs of the City traffic.

The Great Western horses are under the superintendence of Captain Milne, and there is a certain army precision and smartness about the management which is not apparent in all railway stables. As much as possible the colours are kept separate, one stable being of greys, another of chestnuts, another of bays, and so on ; and right well do the carefully groomed animals look, standing in their neat straw litter, with a glint of sunlight on them, clean as a picture against the white background leading up to the varnished pine roof overhead, while most of the smooth arched blue brick gangways are as clean as a man-o'-war deck, the only thing on them being the two fodder sacks, like a huge ottoman, at the far end.

The railway spirit peeps out in the use of obsolete rails for building purposes, two together forming each of the roof pillars, and others laid end to end doing duty as channels, and having the great advantage over brick and stone gutters of being unbreakable. In some of the older stables travises are used, but as a rule the horses stand between swinging bales, or rather double bales—for each has its kicker hung on to the chains with a slip-hook, so as to clear a leg immediately should it get over—and this Reliance hook, which is also on the harness, has proved itself of great value in cases of accident here, in the stable, and in the street.

Over each horse's head is his number, answering to the number branded on his hoof, and behind him is his harness, all in due order as if it were a trooper's ; but there is not a collar to be seen. When the Great Western horse comes home at night his collar goes not to the stable but to the drying-room, whence it comes in the morning ready for wear, warm and comfortable as a clean pair of socks.

At two o'clock on Monday morning the week's work begins. The Covent Garden vans then go out. At eight o'clock the stables are in full bustle, and the runs that slope from floor to floor are alive with the descending crowd, as, to the jingle of the harness, they come cautiously down. Some of them, before the day is out, will have been as far as Woolwich Dockyard and back ; some of them will be out for eighteen hours, to rest on the morrow, some of them for six, to take a longer turn next day. So many vans have to be horsed, and so much work has to be done, and somehow it has to be got through, or there would be an accumulation which it would be difficult to deal with. Early on the Monday morning the silent goods-yard surlily wakes to life, and it knows no rest till Saturday night. What the trains bring the vans must take, what the vans bring the trains must take, be it much or little. Of course there is an average ; and provision is made for the tide which begins to rise at Michaelmas and breaks its last big wave at Easter.

The heaviest railway van weighs two tons, and will carry seven or more. Such a van, with its load drawn by its four-horse team, will be a moving mass of thirteen tons, one of the heaviest things going through the streets of London, as the railway parcels cart is one of the fastest. The team walks; the single horse trots, and is not supposed to go more than eight miles an hour, but he does, although it is not every one who would give him credit for the rate at which he slips along. There is no vehicle in the Great Western service worked with that most extravagant arrangement, a tandem team, but some of the heavy drays have three horses abreast, an economical device, giving almost the power of four horses in two-and-two, and having only the disadvantage of heating the middle horse rather more than the outsiders. Like the fours, and threes, and unicorns, the pairs are supposed to walk, and it is these vans which do most of the work. Their average tare is a ton. Like a train, they are fitted with a powerful brake, which eases the strain of the stoppages, but the starting pull is at times tremendous, particularly with thoughtless drivers, and it is this effort, as much as the constant jarring of the feet, which makes a horse's London life so short.

The railway horse is a farmer's horse to begin with, and for the first two years does practically nothing but grow; in the next two or three years he passes into the regular routine of farm work, and gets into shape; and then he changes masters and comes to London. But as it would not do to take a horse direct from a

Gloucestershire field and place him in the thick of Cheapside, a gradual process of acclimatisation is begun, averaging about two months, during which he is trained to his surroundings and his full work. Sometimes the horse is older when he is bought, but no railway company now buys a horse over seven years of age.

The horses last according to the traffic, the heavier lines with the heavier traffic wearing out their horses more quickly than the southerly lines, whose traffic is mainly in parcels. The Great Western average is five years; the Midland, over a stud of 1,350, is also five; but curiously enough, the Great Northern's, with a stud of 1,300, is but four. This average is, of course, to a certain extent, a matter of policy; it may suit one company to cast its horses earlier than another in order to sell them better, and this consideration renders any comparison of company with company of little value. There is interest in it, notwithstanding, particularly in this case, for the Great Northern endeavours to work its trotting horses only four days a week, and its walking horses five, though both kinds are in harness twelve hours a day. When the Northern horse is done with he is sold for the country or less hard work, like the Midland and others. What he then fetches we do not know, but the Midlander averages 10*l.*, and the Brighton cart horse averages 12*l.* 6*s.* The Brighton work is light and the life rate is high. In its stud of 225 horses the average service is just over seven years, and considering the chances of accident and disease, and above all things, the price obtained at the clearance, the Brighton horse seems to be as well looked after as the Brighton engine. The South Eastern does very similar work with its stud

of 275, but the average service is a year less. The
South Western, with more of heavier work and just
double the stud, makes its horses last for six years and
a half—a remarkably good average.

The Great Western does not send its old horses to
the auctioneer. As many as possible it keeps in a
veteran stable near its goods yard, and it uses them as
helps in dragging the vans up the steep gradients at
the station, which are steeper than any the teams meet
with on their travels. If a team can pull a load out of
Paddington it can take it anywhere in the streets of
London.

Weather will age a horse more than it will a man,
owing to its affecting the work so much; and it will be
quite as prejudicial to its health. In dry weather almost
as many horses slip down as in the rain, and quite as
many are run into; but the dry weather has nothing
to answer for in the way of the chafings by the wet
harness, and the colds and sore throats which lead on
to other troubles that make short work of the London
horse of all sorts and conditions.

If the railway horse could choose its track, it would
never have anything else than good macadam, but the
London traffic is far too great to admit of a macadamised
road remaining in condition for more than a fortnight,
and hence the many substitutes. There is an individu-
ality about the most mechanical 'machiner,' particularly
apparent in the way he wears his shoes, which, as usual
with London horses in hard work, have to be changed
at the rate of one a week, or, to put it more clearly, at
the rate of a set every four weeks. It is rare for two
horses, even in a four-horse team, to wear out their

GREAT WESTERN RAILWAY VAN HORSES

shoes in the same way or in the same order, and with
regard to order alone, the twenty-four possible permu-
tations of the one set of four shoes are all met with in
London farriery practice.   And as some horses will
wear out their shoes far faster than others, so some will
slip and some will fall oftener ; and more human than
all, some horses admirable in every other respect will
meet with constant ill luck.

The majority of London railway horses work about
seventy hours a week ; some, as we have seen, work
less.   The Midland system is to have a limit of fourteen
hours for any one day's work, and owing to this, a
third of its horses are in the stables every week-day, including, of course, the sick and injured, which, however,
form a very small proportion of the stud.   The London
centre is in King's Road, St. Pancras, but the headquarters of the department are at Derby, just as the
headquarters of the provender department are at
Wellingborough, from which the mixture of oats, maize,
beans, hay, and bran, used as food, comes up to London.
The Midland does all its own horse work ; it even,
unlike most other lines, horses its own omnibuses ; but
then the railway omnibus, like third-class expresses,
Pullman cars, and a score of other improvements, was
of Midland introduction, and these 'bus horses are the
best and most costly in the world.   But although the
Midland scorns to be contracted for, it does not object
to supply horse power on contract, and, as a matter of
fact, ninety-six of its stud are at work on hire delivering Bass's beer to the publicans of London.

Its work is more decentralised than that of other
companies.   It has over two hundred horses in King's

Road, at St. Pancras station there are four hundred, and
some it has at Poplar, and some at Kentish Town, and
some for the City at Whitecross Street; and in only one
place are the horses on two floors, so that its stables
cover a good deal of ground. Every sick horse goes to
King's Road, and is there changed for a sound one, in
order that the branch studs may always be in full
efficiency. If an accident happens in the streets, the
boy—that wonderful boy, whose lifting feats are often
so painfully startling—goes off in a cab to the nearest
depôt and brings the relief. And at that depôt he frequently appears under other circumstances delightfully
significant in these days of competition.

The less a man knows of a horse the greater is his
idea of its powers. If the stableman knows more than
the driver on this subject, much greater is the driver's
knowledge than that of the customer from whom he
collects his goods. If a railway van is sent for, it is
rare indeed that it is not expected to take away all the
stuff that can be stacked upon it, quite irrespective of
that stuff's specific gravity. There are some people
who would pile on bag after bag of iron bolts as if they
were pockets of hops; there is no mercy in the London
collecting trade; 'Take the lot' is the motto, and if a
company's van once moves off without taking all the
goods as requested, the remainder will invariably be
given to another company, who will get the chance of
'taking the lot' next time, and for as long afterwards
as their driver is wise enough to stay at the warehouse
door till he has loaded up all remainders. Here then
it is that the judicious driver has his chance, and the
boy is to the front. Off goes the boy to the depôt for

help, and if the loading is over before he comes back, and the police interfere, the bystander will see the heavily laden van dragged off to linger in the nearest bye-street until the arrival of the expected relief.

The average in the railway service is one man to every three horses; but this includes the driver and the boy, who do not properly belong to the horse department, and have nothing to do with the horse except when it is in harness. In the Great Western service the driver is as much as possible given the same horses day after day, but this practice is not general with the Midland men, owing to the way in which the working hours are arranged, and it is only the twenty big waggoners which are associated with particular drivers.

The Midland own more horses than any railway company in London. The stud of the North Western is curiously small; but then the North Western does nearly half its work through its agents. Of its 650 horses three hundred and more are under Broad Street Station, where they form not the least of the nightly attractions of that busy goods depôt. The mention of the North Western agents—who are Messrs. Pickford & Co.—naturally leads us on to the carriers, generally so-called, who are still indispensable as railway feeders and distributors, and in what we may call the retail deliveries between the different parts of the metropolis.

Pickfords do an enormous business, and have a stud of some 4,000 horses, of which about two out of ten pass through their stables in a year. The firm has a long pedigree, and dates back to the days of their old team waggons, the driver of which did not ride on the vehicle, but on a handy cob, from whose back he worked

THE SHUNTER'S HORSE

the string of horses by means of a long whip. One of
the first of these drivers was the founder of the oldest
firm of shipping carriers in London, John Smither &
Co.; and this reminds us that just as the goods-yards
have their feeders and distributors, so have the wharves
and docks. Some of these shipping horses are as good
as those in the railway service, but as a rule they are
of poorer quality. Some are doing their twenty-five
miles a day, and in one stud there is a horse that is
twenty-five years old, but their average London life is
six years; and they are bought at six, when they can
be got at a profitable price. All of them are English,
for in this, as in all other trades where hard work
has to be done, it is the old story of no foreigners need
apply.

Beyond the shipping firms there are what may be
called general carmen and cartage agents, who have
a very miscellaneous connection; and, in addition to
this internal traffic, a certain amount of long-distance
carrying is still done between London and a few towns
and villages in the home counties by the men who start
from the Old Bailey, the One Swan, the Borough Spur,
the Aldgate Saracen's Head, and Spitalfields; but these
have only about 250 horses amongst them, worth say
25*l.* apiece, which can very well be thrown in under the
same heading as those of the larger firms, although they
will not improve our average.

And over and above all these are the few firms whose
names as carriers are household words. The largest of
these is Carter Paterson's, who have a stud of 2,000
stabled at their twenty London depôts, the headquarters
being in the Goswell Road. The system on which

these carrying companies work is practically that of the railways. The parcels are collected from the senders on information received at the numerous order stations, which the public know by the show-boards. From the houses and shops of the consignors the parcels are taken as a rule by one-horse vans to the nearest depôt, where they are transhipped into vans drawn by pairs or teams, and find their way across London to the depôt nearest the address of the consignee, from which depôt they are sent out to their destination in the local single-horse vans.

The headquarters of Carter Paterson's network of traffic is like a railway goods-yard, with the usual ' banks,' as the platforms are called, with their topographical divisions, their truckloads of cans, and barrels, and boxes, and packages, and baths, and perambulators, meandering among other piles of similar miscellaneous character as they are scattered out from one van and gathered from all points for another ; the same sorting, and checking, and sheets—only it is all sheets in this business—in short, the same surroundings, and belongings, and proceedings, except that there are no trucks, and that the goods are somewhat lighter, as we have already noted together in our *Everyday Life on the Railroad.*[1]

The stables are on three floors, one over the other, clean and roomy, each horse by himself, the fixed travis here taking the place of the now more customary bale, so that there is not that close line of backs and tails characteristic of the modern working stable. The

[1] See *Everyday Life on the Railroad*, a companion volume of *The Leisure Hour Library.*

horses are generally of a lighter type than the railway horse, as befits the lighter trade, and they are worked on a different system. Sunday is the rest day, and the horse does nine trips a week; one day he has two trips, the next day he has one, the next he has two, the next one, and so on—three trips every two days. The length of the trip depends very much on the season, and during the fever heat of Christmas time the carrier's horse has quite as much work to do as he can manage.

Then it is that the parcels companies rejoice at the limits of the Parcel Post. The fact of the Post Office not collecting and its refusing everything over eleven pounds of course keeps these busy all the year round; but at Christmas they get the full benefit of the six-foot limits of 'length and girth combined.' To them falls the crowd of immeasurables; and looking at the queer shapes they carry, we can easily understand why it is that the senders have given up length and girth measurement in despair. The parcels trade is then enormous, but so well is it organised that out of the millions of packages of all shapes, weights, and sizes carried by Carter Paterson in a year, only one in 10,000 goes wrong.

This small proportion means, however, a large accumulation, and the lost property department at Goswell Road is instructive not only as regards the peculiar sort of address and packing people think sufficient, but as regards the very varied character of a London carrying business. The staple of the trade seems to be servants' boxes—the shillings collected from the nomadic domestic must amount to thousands of pounds in the course of the year—but one is hardly prepared for the cases of eggs 'refused delivery,' probably on account of the too obviously advanced 'shop 'un' quality of their contents, the iron bedsteads gone astray, the baths, garden tools, bundles of bedding, washstands, dog-kennels, iron bars, bicycles, perambulators, chairs, china, fruit, and boots and shoes which here find themselves together awaiting an owner.

The load of the carrier's horse is thus cumbrous rather than weighty; the vehicles range from the box furniture van to the parcels cart, and it is not often that the ton and a half which is the maximum an ordinary horse should have to draw on London streets is exceeded.

Pickfords, who do heavier work in connection with the North Western, and the other firms who have a good deal of railway agency, have heavier horses to suit the trade. One of the noticeable things on Thanksgiving Day in 1872 was the ease with which the Speaker's coach, usually drawn by six horses, was hauled along by a pair of Pickford's Clydesdales, engaged for that occasion only, behind whom it seemed to be as light as an empty dray. The Parcels Delivery Company are at the other end of the scale, and average a much lighter build of animal; in fact, the carrier's horse is of all varieties, down to the Old Bailey screw, and we may as well say beyond, for London has worse horses in a carrier's cart than those that start from the King of Denmark and the Lamb, and occasionally a really good specimen will be seen among the waggons and tilt carts that still rendezvous at London's old Place de la Grève.

E

DELIVERY VANS IN FLEET STREET

Some of them are evidently of an advanced age, but then it is not every carrier's horse that has made its first appearance in London in that character. The more hours they rest the longer they last, and the more they fetch when 'cast'; but in a good many instances the casting is the final one to that dark bourne whence no horse returns except as 'meat.' These, however, are the great minority; the majority having yet another, and perhaps another, experience before they face the slaughterman. Some last a few months; of others there are very extraordinary stories, but we refrain; and even including the patriarchs, we should not have an average of much more than five years of London hard labour.

There are about 19,000 of them in all, and these are of all grades, from the excellent to the indifferent— the latter, as in the case of the cab horses, being the exception and not the rule. The price paid for the lot when they first entered the carrying business must have been very close on 900,000*l.*, and supposing each horse costs twelve shillings a week to feed—which he does at the least—it must take about 600,000*l.* a year to keep them going, independently of what it may cost to attend to them, to drive them, and to house them.

Including the railways, we have thus in our metropolitan carrying trade some 25,000 horses, worth 1,260,000*l.*, and costing 800,000*l.* a year for food alone. And adding these to the omnibus horses, tram horses, and cab horses already dealt with, we have found in London an equine herd of 72,000. And we have thousands more to follow.

THE ROYAL PARCEL MAIL

CHAPTER IV

THE POST-OFFICE HORSE

FROM the carrier's cart it is but a step to the Post-Office van. The Post Office owns no horses; it does its work by contract, and McNamara's have 'horsed the mails' ever since that *annus mirabilis* 1837, when so many good things began.

They have now 600 horses at their central quarters in Finsbury and the local branches from which the outer ring of postal districts is worked, besides a few hundred others for trade traffic. And out of London there are forty-two horses on the Brighton road working the Parcels Coach, and the twenty-six Tunbridge Wells Coach horses, and the other coach horses; but these cannot fairly come into our census, except as regards those for the first stage out and last stage home —the stages being the ten-mile ones of 'the gloricus old coaching-days,' concerning which we may have something to say presently.

The mail horse is the least conspicuous of draught animals. How often do we hear a shout of 'Here comes the mail!' and how seldom do we trouble as to what its horses are like! Our attention is caught and fixed by the scarlet cart, while horse and man pass

unnoticed; scarlet will have its way, and a mass of it
in movement throws all its surroundings into background. Not that the horse need fear criticism. At
times he is somewhat rough, at others a trifle weedy;
but, taking him by the hundred, he is a serviceable
servant, with no nonsense about him, and rarely much
to find fault with. Like most of his brethren, he
makes his first appearance in the London streets
between his fifth and seventh years. Younger than
five, no wise master will have a horse for London
cartage work. 'Under that age,' as an authority told
us, 'they are like children and catch every ailment that
comes along.'

The Post-Office horse is always at work. What
with 'mails inwards' in the morning, 'mails inter-
changeable' during the day, and 'mails outwards' at
night, and 'foreign mails' arriving before their time
at all hours of the day and night, and which he must
always be at the railway to meet, he has quite enough
to employ and worry him. He begins his week's work
at four o'clock on Sunday afternoon; he ends it at half-
past ten on Sunday morning; and at any time during
that long week he is liable for instant service, and has
only five and a half hours' undisturbed rest. Of course
he gets a good deal more as he becomes used to the
bustle of the stable, but that is the only respite he is
sure of—just enough, as it were, to go to church and
digest the Sunday's dinner. And yet with all this,
while the tram horse is cast after four years, and the
omnibus horse after five, the mail horse is not weeded
out of the service until on an average he has spent six
in it.

He is generally English, but comes from no county in particular, and costs rather more than the omnibus horse, for we shall be averaging him rather under the mark at 36*l.* ; but he is well looked after and has few ailments. It is not often that a mail horse is sick or goes very wrong. At every railway station to which he goes there is a foreman to look after him, and at every stable there is a keeper to every dozen horses, so that he is attended to at both ends, and his keepers check each other to his advantage. And he lives, as a rule, in flats, in an atmosphere of disinfectants and a continual round of whitewashing; so that everything is done to keep him in health, and the result justifies the effort.

And he is fed well—indeed, if he were not, he could not stand the work. One of the noticeable things at the ever-extending headquarters in Castle Street is the mixing machine, in which the oats and clover and hay and beans are blended into the general mass which forms the fodder. On one floor the hay and clover are being chopped by steam, the knives, owing to the silex in the straw, requiring renewal every twenty minutes; on another floor the chopped stuff is being poured into hoppers sackful by sackful; on another, oats are being poured into another hopper, beans into another; and all these hoppers communicate with channels and spiral travellers and ingenious mixers, so that in the delivery the blend is even and free from all patchiness—the last stage being when the mixture is shot into a huge bin, the bottom of which is, by a turn of a lever, converted into so many swing-fans, between which the provender falls instantly into the sacks below.

McNamara's not only mix their own fodder, but make their own harness, their own shoes, their own wheels, and even their own carts—for the mail carts are not designed by the Post Office, but by the contractors, and then built on approval. The body of a one-horse mail cart looks not unlike a cupboard until it gets the wheels on, but it is rather more elaborate in its decoration, simple as it may seem, for before it gains the royal colour which saves the horse from notice it requires no less than sixteen different coats of paint and varnish. There are 260 of these red carts and vans, and the yard is busy with them and the parcel coaches coming in splashed and thick with mud—the coaches having been out all night, to remain till night, and the carts having most of them been out since four in the morning, and being off again with the change horse.

In and out the horses are worked with very little attempt at a hard-and-fast routine, owing to the irregularity in time and bulk of the foreign mails, which forms the great difficulty of the business, and makes the problem to be dealt with that of dealing with surprise trains. The unexpectedness of these is due to the limit being made as wide as possible at the shipping company's request, in order to save them from all risk of penalty for being behind-hand, and the arrival taking place as far as possible within the limit, for the sake of the company's reputation. The inland mail that comes to the moment can be provided for as easily as the outgoing mail that starts to its time; it is the foreign mail brought by the record-breaker, and delivered any number of hours before it is due, for which the Post-Office horse has to suffer.

Like the omnibus horse, the tram horse, the cab horse, and the carrier's horse, the profit from his work is direct. The railway horses we have grouped under the same heading, although it is open for any one to say that they are only used for the purpose of collecting traffic for the rail, and consequently can be worked so as to save a loss. But railway companies are merely tradesmen on a large scale, and no tradesman keeps a horse unless he hopes to gain some pecuniary advantage by doing so. The only horses worked at a loss are pleasure horses, such as are used by carriage people and equestrians; but these form a class by themselves, and with the livery section, can wait a while.

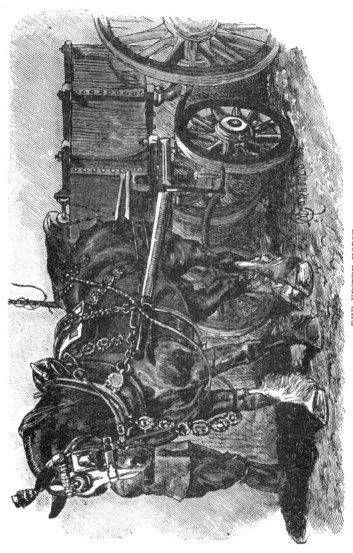

THE VESTRY HORSE

CHAPTER V

THE VESTRY HORSE

THE Parcel Post led us to digress among the mail horses; let us return to the heavy brigade. But we must clear as we go, and as there happens to be a class of cart-horse holding a position by himself, let us deal with him forthwith. Although he is employed for the saving of money, he is to a large extent of superior quality, owing to the pressure of appearances. With him there is, to put it gently, just a little more than a suspicion of 'nobility compels,' and that honourable compulsion is at the expense of the community.

The thirteen hundred thousand cart-loads of refuse removed from London in a year[1] require a small horde of about 1,500 horses to deal with them, and of these more than half now belong to the vestries and district Boards of Works. What may be called the 'municipal horse' is a really good cart-horse. Any approach to 'the vanner' will not suit the vestries. His load varies too much, even with similar stuff, for any risks to be run. On a wet day he may have three tons behind him, including the vehicle; on a fine day the absence of the

---

[1] See *How London Lives,* in *The Leisure Hour Library*, published at 56 Paternoster Row.

water will take hundredweights off the weight, to say
nothing of the improvement in the state of the road.

Some of these vestry horses we have seen weigh
over 18 cwt., and, though we have heard of a few
heavier, we heard of none lighter than 13½ cwt., the
average working out at 17 cwt.—rather over than
under. Such horses are now all English, coming from
almost every county, direct from the farmer or through
the dealer, and with very few exceptions they are
bought in their sixth year.

No foreign horse will live long in the London dust-
cart; his feet will not stand the hard roads. He has
been tried, and failed miserably, giving way in the forelegs, having strained the back tendons with the constant
jar of his feet as he has plodded along on the granite,
asphalt, or wood. And this has been particularly
noticeable in the City service, where the only stretch of
macadam is that between Lett's Wharf and Blackfriars
Bridge, which is not in the City at all, although it leads
to the City dust-yard.

And it is not every sound horse, however big and
handsome, that will suit the vestry. He has to possess
an accomplishment which he is little used to display
in the country. It will not do for him to be of the
vestigia nulla retrorsum school, he must not only go
forward, he must above all things be able to ' back,'
and he must back as readily as he advances. When
he is bought he is tried and drilled in this backing;
and he must not only back, but keep in his legs as he
does so, for if not his career will be cut short by his
having his feet run over, which is the commonest
accident to which he is liable when standing in the

London streets. The performances of some of these animals in backing and turning are remarkable. There was one mare, a year or so ago, who used to work in Bucklersbury, where it often became necessary for her to turn round. Now, Bucklersbury is a narrow thoroughfare, and to turn in it the mare had to get on to the pavement, in which, here and there, are cellar lights; and it was quite a lesson to watch her come round, carefully picking her way so as not to tread on the glass lights, which she had learnt to consider dangerous.

Many of the horses are mares, but most of them are geldings; most of these are bays, many of them are roans, and the blue roans are said to last the best, which may be a mistake, although there is little doubt that the rat-tailed ones of any colour last the longest. The average working life in the vestry service is eight years; when they are sold out of it they fetch on the average 8*l*. if alive, and 1*l*. 18*s*. if dead. But their death rate is not high; indeed, among the City horses, which number between eighty and ninety, only one horse has died in every three months during the last twenty years.

The average price now paid for them is 75*l*., and a few cost over 80*l*.; but though London has many fine animals among the vestry studs, such as those owned by Marylebone, Battersea, St. George's Hanover Square, and Kensington—the four prize-winners at a recent Cart-horse Parade—there are some we have heard of worth three figures, although the value of heavy draught horses is always on the rise.

It is rather puzzling to find that while the amount

of land going out of cultivation increases, the number
of horses supposed to work on that land also increases ;
but the solution of the mystery is that not only are
horse implements taking the place of men, but that it
pays the farmer better to breed horses than to plough
with them, particularly as the more he breeds the
better price he seems to sell them at.   The farmer
suffers as much as most men from foreign competition,
but as a horse breeder it is by foreign competition that
he benefits.   And according to the users of horseflesh
he benefits most by the increasing number of horse and
agricultural shows.   For some years now, for instance,
the Americans have been buying shire horses of good
quality.   Shows are plentiful, and at every show the
American agent puts in an appearance, endeavouring
at all cost to secure the prize-winners, and thus have
the best of opinions to back up his own.   His own
judgment might land him in difficulties with his
correspondents, but with the prize certificate he is safe.
' In any court of law he would get a verdict,' we were
told by one of the best judges of cart-horses in
London ; ' and if he were to send his people a three-
cornered horse, they couldn't quarrel with him ! '   But
as this excellent method of picking out a good horse
is not confined to Americans, prize-winners fetch high
prices ; and even though the winners go out of the
country, the farmer benefits by the price, and the
country benefits by the breeding of good horses in the
hope of obtaining that price.

And even beyond this the horse societies have
certainly justified their existence in the prices now obtainable for breeding stock.   Not long ago men won-

dered at a champion stallion like Enterprise of Cannock being sold for a thousand guineas; but since then we have had Prince William changing hands at fifteen hundred guineas; and now that price has been far exceeded in the case of Bury Victor Chief, the two-year-old shire stallion, who was bought out of Huntingdonshire by Mr. Wainwright, of Chapel-en-le-Frith, for the handsome sum of two thousand five hundred guineas—2,625*l.* for a draught horse, who is expected to pay for himself in three seasons, during which insurance will cover the risk!

But as we are not likely to meet with a two-thousand-five-hundred-guinea stallion in a vestry stable, we will say no more about him. When the five-year-old horse arrives in London, he almost invariably falls sick, and takes at least a week to become acclimatised and used to his surroundings. He is then exercised in backing, and when he has duly passed in this important part of his drill, he is put to light work for a week or so, bringing in a load a day. When he has acquired confidence and is thoroughly fit, he is placed in charge of a driver, with whom, if he gets on well, he will stay until either horse or master leaves the service. Some consideration is needed in fitting a man with a horse. A short man with a choppy step will never be comfortable with a free striding horse, and a man who lounges along with a leisurely swing will always be in difficulties with a quick mover. The gait of horse and man must be somewhat similar, and as they begin to know and take an interest in each other, it is astonishing how much alike they will become in their movements.

The vestry horse, as a rule, begins work at six o'clock on Monday morning, and knocks off at five o'clock on Saturday night, so that he has a full day's rest once a week. Every day he begins at six, and works about eleven hours, bringing in two or three loads during that time, each load averaging about two and a half tons, taking the twelve months round; but most of his time is spent in standing about accumulating this load, so that he cannot be said to be overworked.

He costs fifteen shillings a week to feed, but his provender varies in different stables. At Lett's Wharf the mixture consists of one truss each of hay and straw to three of clover and half a dozen bushels of oats; and of this each horse has forty pounds a day. He has his breakfast at three o'clock in the morning, and takes out a nosebag with him on each journey; sometimes he has a feed of beans or some special mixture; and invariably he has a bran mash to wind up the week with on Saturday night.

When he comes in wet and dirty a bale of peat moss is broken for him to stand in, and in this he is thoroughly groomed before he goes to the stable; and he goes to the stall at the word of command, knowing his place quite as well as the horsekeeper. And if he is a City horse, his stall is roomy and lofty—no swinging bales for him, although he stands not on straw, but on the more economical peat. He lives in good condition, for his driver gets a bonus of a sovereign or two every year for keeping him so; and he rarely comes to grief in the streets, owing to his driver being by his side to warn him when the paving changes, and check him generally. And nails rarely trouble him, as he seldom is leg-weary, and he treads on such a gathering of rubbish in the dust-yard, that he gets quite experienced in dealing with the odds and ends he meets with on the roadway.

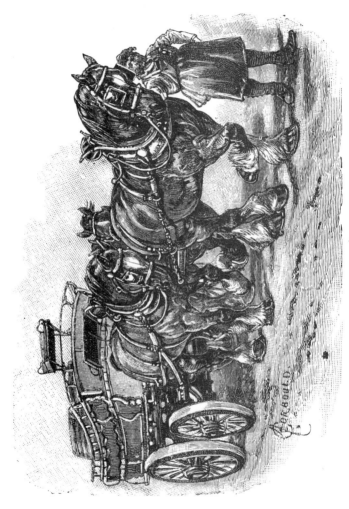

THE BREWER'S HORSE

CHAPTER VI

THE BREWER'S HORSE

VERY different is the brewer's horse from the vestry animal, which is of very much the same class. He picks up as many nails as any horse in London, and at one brewery we saw a tin box full of small ironmongery brought home in horses' feet. ' Whenever a house is pulled down,' said the horse-keeper to us, ' there is danger to the feet of the horses that pass along the road. When property is being demolished in this neighbourhood, I send the teams a little way round, to avoid passing by it if they possibly can. People have no idea of the extraordinary things a horse's foot will hold. Look there, and there!' and out of the box he took a 4-inch brass thumb-screw, and an awkwardly broken link of a thick iron chain.

The brewer's horse is a splendid animal, the most powerful as a rule of London's heavy brigade. At the Cart-horse Parade, in which teams of all classes compete, the first, second, and third prizes were taken for the only two years in which they entered by Messrs. Courage, whose cast horses are generally sold for an average of 32l. each, one of them having fetched fifty-one guineas, the highest price ever obtained for a horse cleared out of a stud as being past the work of the trade in which he made his first appearance in town. In fact, there is no stud in the kingdom of higher level excellence than that under Mr. Laird's care at Horselydown, which is saying much, considering that the 3,000 horses owned by the larger London brewers are worth at the very lowest estimate 90*l*. apiece.

A barrel of beer weighs 4 cwt. ; a brewer's van carries 25 barrels, which means 5 tons ; the van itself weighs not less than 35 cwt., some of them weigh over 2 tons ; the harness weighs three quarters of a hundredweight ; the men weigh—what ? It is a delicate question. To answer it Mr. Laird weighed a drayman for us, a fine young man in his twenty-ninth year. He weighed 20 st. 10 lbs. ! And the horse he drove, a five-year-old gelding standing 17·2 and still growing, was then put on the scale, and dipped the beam at just over the ton.

But this is hardly a fair average. Let us throw the men in with the sundries, and say these tremendous horses have to draw 8 tons ; and this is for three horses worked unicorn fashion, two at the pole and one as leader. According to one horse-keeper, who had been twenty-seven years in his position, it now takes three horses to do the work that four did twenty years ago. ' The vans have improved, the roads have improved, and the horses have improved, especially the horses ' ; but this is not the usual opinion, for even with the brewer's horse the laudation of the past is the consolation of the many.

Sir Walter Gilbey has shown that the shire horse is the survival of the Great War Horse of the armoured knights, and that that horse in the days of Henry VIII. carried 4 cwt. on his back. When armour went out of fashion the war-horse went to the plough, and eventually, like most agricultural labourers, came in great numbers into the towns; but that he is degenerating is doubtful; and we will undertake to say that there is not a horse in Courage's stables that would not easily carry Charles Brandon with all his 90 lbs. of man's armour, and 80 lbs. of horse armour—including a few gallons of beer for the knight's refreshment.

On most of these horses there is not a pound of superfluous flesh. They are working regularly every week-day, doing often their fourteen hours a day, sometimes doing sixteen hours, resting on Sundays, and having a light load on Monday, which is the brewer's dull day; out at five o'clock in the morning, back into stable at seven at night; averaging six years of work; and then, in many cases, realising over 20*l.* under the hammer when cleared out to make way for the newcomers.

Most of those under notice to quit look little the worse for wear, although perhaps their legs may have come over a little with the draught, which in the suburbs is severe, the load being no light one to drag over a hilly track at the brewer's walking rate of five miles an hour easy. But it does not do for a team to have a weak horse, unless, maybe, the leader, who can shirk now and then if he chooses, for the rate of the slowest is ever the rate of progress; hence horses are worked together only so long as they work equally, and the weak one is rejected immediately he is found out, lest he should demoralise his companions.

There is a prevalent notion that hairy-legged horses
stand heavy work better than others, but the value is
not in the hair, but in the stout bone it should cover.
One of Courage's best horses is a Clydesdale, with his
fore legs so fine, because fleshless and so thinly-haired,
that the question has been asked if it was intended 'to
go racing with that animal'; but Clydesdales, though
now improving every year, do not run quite heavy
enough for brewers' work, and nearly all the horses are
shires. Some brewers—Barclay & Perkins, for instance
—have nothing but shires in their stables; and this
particular stud, a singularly fine one, averages seven
and a half years of brewery life.

Of course all the brewers do not work their horses
on the same system. Hoare's, by way of example, work
their 160 horses only five days a week, and no horse is
allowed to be out more than ten hours without being
examined by the horse-keeper. Their horses are bought
at six years old and cleared out on the average at twelve,
which is as soon as they show the least sign of decay ;
and there is not a horse in their stud weighing under
16 cwt. or standing under 17 hands, which compares
rather awkwardly for the antiquarians with the 14
'handfuls' which Henry VIII. fixed as the minimum of
stallions in 1535. A range of twelve inches, unless the
horses were of very different classes, seems too wide to
be true.   The thoroughbred racehorse increases a
hand in height every century ; in 1700 he stood 13·2,
he now stands 15·2 ; and it certainly looks as though
the heavy horse had also grown a little.

It is noteworthy that these big horses should so very
seldom have bad tempers ; they are almost as intelli-

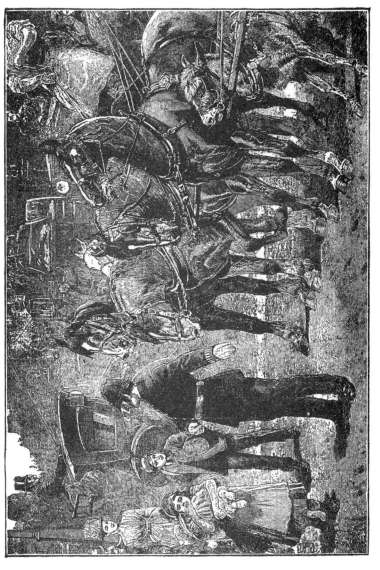

THE REIGN OF LAW!

gent as dogs, and quite as amiable. They are in rude
health, it is true, and that may account for their being
comfortable and pleased with themselves, more especially as they are kept hard at regular work, but it is
scarcely enough to answer for their peculiar placidity
under all circumstances.

The one great secret of keeping them in condition
is attention to their feet. There is no animal more
carefully shod than a brewer's horse. Many of them
have a different make and shape of shoe on each hoof.
At Courage's, for instance, no such things as standard
sizes are known ; the shoe is always made specially to fit
the foot, and the shoes are never thrown away, but are
mended—soled and heeled, in fact—by having pieces of
iron welded into them again and again as they are worn.
Some of the shoes are steel-faced ; some are barred, the
shoe going all round the foot ; some have heels, some
have toes ; some have one clip, some have two ; in fact,
there are almost as many makes of shoe as there are in
a Northampton factory.

But enough of the brewer's horse. His food is not
grains, but combinations of the best of clover, hay,
sainfoin, straw, and oats, with in some places a little
maize, in others a few beans—nothing out of the way,
in fact, except in quantity. He begins to eat very
early in the morning—there is one stable where he
takes his breakfast at 2 A.M.—and he eats nearly
eighteen shillings' worth a week. When the time
comes for his final retirement from the worldly stage he
is worth much the same as the vestry horse. But stay.
He does not always go to the knacker's. A recent
walk along the riverside revealed the fact that, like

many another horse who has had his day, he is ' exported.'
Exported to America ? To France ? No. To Ham-
burg; whence he is reported to return, lost in the
oblivion of sausage meat, and labelled ' made in
Germany.'

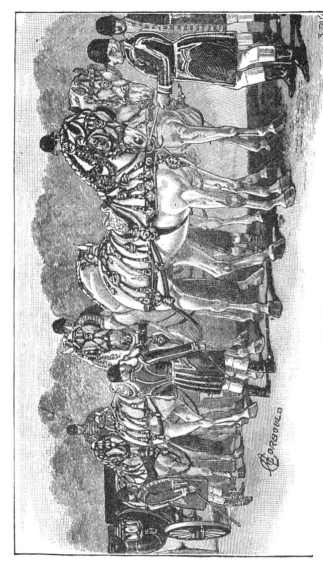

THE QUEEN'S CREAMS

CHAPTER VII

THE QUEEN'S HORSE

In the horse-world of London, the highest circle, the most exclusive set, so to speak, is that housed at Buckingham Palace. To many loyal subjects the Queen's horses are as much an object of interest as the regalia; and as cards of admission are freely granted by the Master of the Horse, the Royal Mews are probably the best known stables within the bills of mortality.

There are in them from ninety to a hundred horses —state horses; harness horses, coach and light; riding horses, and what not—whose forage bill runs into 30 quarters of corn, $3\frac{1}{2}$ loads of hay, and $3\frac{1}{2}$ loads of straw a week. Immediately to the right of the entrance gate is a stable for ten horses, mostly light and used in ordinary work; to the left is a similar stable similarly occupied. On the east side of the quadrangle are the coaches, state and semi-state, and, among others, the Jubilee landau. On the west side are more horses— sixteen or twenty of them. The state stables for the creams and blacks are on the north side, and to the left of them are housed the thirty-two splendid bays, many of them bred at the Queen's stud farm at Hampton

Court ; the rest bought from the dealers at prices
ranging from 180*l.* to 200*l.*　Stables there are in
London of more aggressive architectural features, and

ROYAL MEWS : ENTRANCE TO QUADRANGLE

some in which there is a far greater show of the very
latest improvements ; but there are none more well-to-
do looking, none in which the occupants seem more at
home.　Comfort and order are everywhere apparent ;

the grooming is, of course, perfection ; and there does not even appear to be a straw out of place in the litter.

To keep a horse in health we are told that he should not stand in a stable giving him less than 1,200 cubic feet of air. The average London private stable gives him only 720 cubic feet ; at the Regent's Park barracks he has 761 cubic feet ; at the new cavalry barracks at Knightsbridge he has 1,781 cubic feet. In the Royal Mews he has 2,500 cubic feet, and as these roomy, comfortable halls average about twenty stalls apiece, the highly-bred harness horse can be seen in them amongst the most favourable surroundings. And so can the riding horse.

The Queen has, however, long given up riding, and the only saddle horses in the stable are those used by the suite. Raikes relates in his journal that a few days after her accession she sent for Lord Albemarle, then Master of the Horse, and said to him, ' My lord, you will immediately provide for me six chargers to review my troops ! ' It is probable that the order was not fully executed, but if it were, matters are managed very differently now.

The Queen has her favourites, and in matters of horseflesh is content to leave well alone as long as possible. If a pair fetches her Majesty from Paddington, it is always the same pair ; if she drives in the Park with four horses, it is always the same team ; so that practically out of the hundred horses the Queen uses but six. The horses ridden by the equerries and outriders are also kept at their special work as long as they are found fit, and the visitor going the round of the stables after an interval of years, will find Black-man, and Phalanx, and Sewell, and their companions still flourishing, and seemingly more conscious than ever of the distinguished success with which they do their duty in the royal equipage of everyday life.

Of a different class altogether are the 'state horses,' which appear only on procession days, and are as much a part of the pageantry of royalty as the crown and sceptre, and other working tools of that degree. These have a stable to themselves, the 'creams' on one side, the 'blacks' on the other. The creams, like the dynasty, are of Hanoverian origin, but they have for generations been of British birth, and, like a large number of the royal horses, first breathed fresh air in the paddocks of Hampton Court. In popular superstition they represent the white horse of Hanover; but that peculiar strain died out long ago, except heraldically, and the creams were always distinct from it. Another erroneous notion, fostered, perhaps, for advertisement purposes, is that the state creams are 'cast' and find their way into circuses; but the only specimens that are ever allowed to quit the palaces go as geldings to the band of the Life Guards. With that one exception, the creams come to London when three years old, and live and are buried in the service in which they are born. Being either entire horses or mares, they require a good deal of attention; they are never left alone by day or night; and the man in charge, who has the highest post in his department, sleeps in the stable, and claims to have the longest day's work in the employment of the State.

Opposite to them are the blacks, which though,

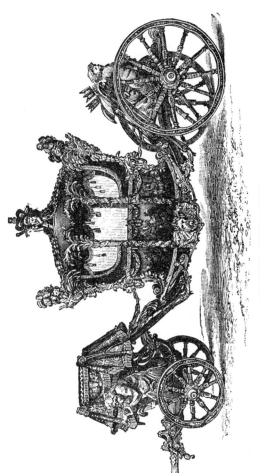

THE ROYAL STATE COACH

perhaps, not so graceful, are more serviceable-looking. They also are of Hanoverian origin, being essentially well-bred specimens of the better class of hearse horse, now rare amongst us owing to the preference given by our undertakers to the more sympathetically lugubrious —and cheaper—Flemish breed. They are big, splendidly showy horses, ' with a power of pride in them.'

Like the creams, they never appear on duty with unplaited manes, the blacks being decked with crimson ribbons, the creams with purple. A trifling matter this of plaiting the manes, but on trifles oft a crown doth hang. Once only did the state creams go forth unplaited. It was in 1831, when Earl Grey and Lord Brougham waited upon William IV. to recommend the immediate dissolution of the Parliament, which was playing havoc with the first Reform Bill. The scruples of the King at dissolving so young a Parliament had all been overcome, and he announced his intention of starting for the Houses forthwith, when it was pointed out that there would be no time to plait the horses' manes. ' Plait the manes !' said his Sailor Majesty, ' then '—with the loudest and, of course, most dignified of expletives—' I'll go in a hackney coach !' Horror of horrors ! the King on such a mission in a hackney coach ! And so the manes were left unplaited, and the State was saved.

But the unplaitedness disturbed many courtly minds, and Mr. Roberts, the King's coachman, above all men, was most indignant. And so it happened that a still more terrible thing took place. The horses had not been out for some time, and being harnessed in a hurry, they were, like their coachman, not in the

placidest of tempers. As they passed the colour party
of the Guards, the ensign, in the usual way, saluted.
The creams took fright at the flash of colour, and broke
into a trot. The great Mr. Roberts began to curse the
soldiers loudly, and tried to check the horses in vain.
On went the coach briskly. ' It was noticed,' say the
contemporary historians, ' that his Majesty proceeded at
a faster rate than usual, in his eagerness to carry out
the wishes of his people,' and, in short, he reached the
Houses considerably before his time. All went smoothly
enough inside, but outside there was anything but
smoothness. The indignant colour-bearers appealed to
their superior officers, and Mr. Roberts had to descend
in double quick time from his exalted perch and humbly
beg pardon for his insult to the outraged Guards.
' Swear at the King's colour, sir! Apologise instantly !'
And he did. And if he had not done so, it is more
than probable that the King would have had to have
called that historical hackney coach for the return
journey, while the unplaited team went home, certainly
Robertsless, if not coachmanless.

Neither the creams nor the blacks have had much
to do of late years. Though they are the leaders of the
London horse-world, their appearances are few ; but they
can be occasionally found taking their exercise in pairs.
The work of all the royal horses is necessarily irregular,
as, though a few may be sent to Windsor, the bulk are
kept continuously in London, and when the Court is
away their occupation is mostly mere exercise. But
when the Court is in town they have quite enough to
do, work in the stables beginning at five o'clock in the
morning, and sometimes, as when the German Emperor

G

THE STATE STABLE

was at the palace, there is no rest until half-past two next morning. The routine is conducted with much more precision than in a private stable. Great care is taken that every turn-out is as it should be, and at every public function the carriages are paraded and inspected in the quadrangle before they are allowed to leave the stable gates.

The weight behind the state team is about equal to that of a loaded pair-horse railway van. The old state coach weighs four tons, that wonderful coach which cost 7,652*l.* 16*s.* 9$\frac{1}{2}$*d.*, out of which 2,500*l.* went to the carver ; the new one weighs a little less. By the 'old' state coach we mean the one made for George III., the one with which the black harness is used ; the present state harness is of red morocco, a remarkably handsome piece of work with its gilt mountings, though it looks rather heavy in the glass case in which, like its predecessor, it is kept hung up to view. But as with the horses and carriages, the harness in everyday wear is in far better taste, and the working harness-room is quite a picture of brilliancy, the steel being kept by the younger servants as bright as the brightest of silver, and showing up at its best on the blue cloth pads.

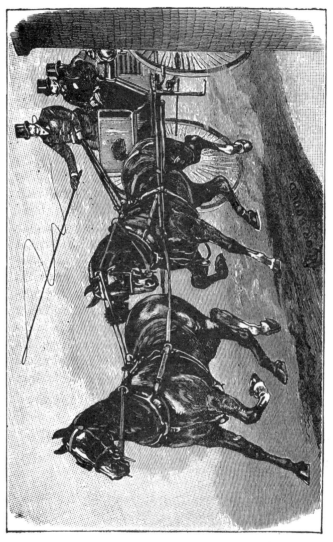

TANDEM

CHAPTER VIII

THE CARRIAGE HORSE

A FOUR-HORSE coach weighs a ton ; a single brougham, the lightest close carriage built, weighs about seven hundredweight : the carriage horse has thus not much of a weight to pull, but he has to pull it at a good pace, and it is the pace that kills. In quick work nowadays it is as much as an average carriage horse can do to travel fourteen miles a day for five days only of the week.

Eighty per cent. of the magnificent animals that draw the family coaches to the Queen's drawing-rooms are on hire from the jobmaster. If you keep them and shoe them yourself at your own stables, you can get them for a hundred guineas a year; if you want them only from April to July, you will be lucky to get them for six guineas a week, taking them by the month; or if you want them in the off season, you can, perhaps, have them cheap at sixteen guineas a month. If the jobmaster keeps them and shoes them at his stables, his charge is nearly double. This is for what is known as ' state coach horses,' but good carriage horses cost as much. Some jobmasters will provide you with brougham and horse, and everything but the coachman's

livery, for 200*l.* a year, but only on the condition that
you never go outside the seven-miles radius from
Charing Cross. In fact, the first-class carriage horse is
a somewhat unsatisfactory investment ; it is safer to
hire than to buy him ; and hence the importance of the
jobmaster in the horse-world of London.

There are some of the London jobmasters with
500 pairs out among the carriage folk, and several with
over a hundred pairs. These horses are nearly all
geldings, and they almost all begin their carriage work
when they are four and a half years old ; if they are
bought before, they have to be kept till fit, which is
another way of saying that there is little monetary
advantage in buying them young, as the cost of their
keep increases their price. Out of each thousand, three
hundred are cleared out of the stables in a year to the
auction mart, and about twenty-five die from accident
or disease.

How many carriage horses are there in London ?
By the courtesy of the Board of Inland Revenue we
are enabled to speak precisely with regard to the number
of carriages. During the year ending March 31, 1891,
the number of carriage licences issued within the
Administrative County of London was 22,204. Of
these, 7,955 were for carriages with four or more wheels
drawn by two or more horses ; 7,535 for carriages with
four or more wheels but fitted to be drawn by one
horse only, and 6,714 for carriages with less than
four wheels. Of course, this is independent altogether
of the hackney carriages which are given in the Metropolitan Police report, and of all vehicles, carts,
vans and otherwise, used in trade. These carriages

ON THE WAY TO THE DRAWING-ROOM

have probably about forty thousand horses, varying
in value from the twenty-guinea pony up to the
four-hundred-guinea state-coach horse; to average
them is almost impossible, although the lot would
certainly represent more than 2,500,000*l.* at present
prices.

There are just double as many private carriages in
London as there are cabs, and they range from the
fifteen-guinea pony trap up to the three-hundred-guinea
chariot, and beyond to the gorgeous official coaches,
including the Lord Mayor's carriage, which pays duty
like the rest. How to sort out the proportions we
candidly do not know, but if we adopt for the
capital they represent the excellent principle suggested by Mr. Montague Tigg, ' and put down a one,
and as many noughts as we can get in the line,' we
shall have a million's worth, and average our vehicles
at 45*l.* each, which is about half what they are generally said to amount to.

Doubling the million, then, and adding to it the
two millions and a half for the horses, and another
half million for the stabling and harness, we arrive
at five millions as the approximate value of the London private carriages and their horses, with their
stables and coach-houses. In the last half million we
are well enough within the mark to allow for any
excess we may have made in the other items, for a
set of pony harness will cost 5*l.*, and much of the
double chariot harness seen in St. James's Street
during a drawing-room is worth from thirty to forty
pounds a set; and for stable accommodation the stock
estimate is 15*l.* per horse.

The stabling in a London mews has not the best of reputations, and its accommodation compares unfavourably with that obtainable at a country town ; in fact, it is owing in a great measure to the stable difficulty that so many people job their horses during the London season. The horse of pleasure is not like the horse of trade ; he is worked at all hours, but rarely with regularity ; he is kept healthy with exercise instead of work ; and consequently he has to be carefully looked after, and wants the best of housing, which in London he does not always get.

A large number of these showy carriage horses are Cleveland bays, bred in North Yorkshire and South Durham, such horses as in recent years have been sold at from 30*l*. to 60*l*. as stud-book foals, at from 50*l*. to 70*l*. as yearlings, and at from 60*l*. to 160*l*. as two-year-olds. At one time the Cleveland mare was almost the only mother of our best carriage horses, but of late a good many of them trace their maternal pedigree through the Clydesdale breed, the result being a gain in hardiness and in the firmness and fitness of the feet for the hard paving of the town streets. But there are thousands which are neither Clevelands nor Clydesdales, and are bred from a Yorkshire coach-horse and a thoroughbred mare, or from the humble hackney stallion and half-bred mare, such as may occasionally be found in our omnibus and van stables. And there are thousands that are not home-bred at all. In every county in England the foreign ' machiner ' will be found ousting the native, and in Hyde Park during the season he will be found in dozens, unmistakable though unlabelled, crawling along as leisurely as if his owner or hirer were like the great Earl of Chesterfield rehearsing a funeral.

Thousands of horses are imported and exported annually. So great is the Continental trade, that at Harwich, for instance, the Great Eastern Railway Company have provided stabling for eighty horses, which is frequently full. As many as 120 have been sent across the sea in one boat, most of them being Irish; indeed, the whole Belgian army used to be horsed from Ireland, the shipments, of course, going direct. We import mostly for the cheaper kinds of work, and we export for hard work, breeding, and waste, and in a whisper be it mentioned, for various food preparations, though not largely for these last. Sometimes the exports exceed the imports; sometimes, and oftener, the balance is the other way; though it is always on the right side as far as cash is concerned, for the imported horses average 17*l*. as their value, while the exported horse is worth 54*l*.

In 1890, 19,400 horses came into this country and 12,900 went out; in 1889, 13,800 came in and 14,200 went out; and in three years the exports realised 2,532,000*l*., while the imports were declared at only 804,000*l*. In 1876, when our horse-world was in a bad way, as many as 40,700 came in, but the imports have ever since shown a tendency downwards. Of these foreigners London has always taken the largest share. They are of all classes. On one occasion Tattersall's sold a batch of carriage horses from the States—good upstanding animals of sixteen hands or more, with good teeth and the uncut tail so much valued by jobmasters for their fashionable hirers, and

these fetched in some cases 80 and 120 guineas. But
the bulk of our imports are not of this quality, and
come from nearer home. The draught horses come in
from Denmark, Holland, Belgium, and France; the
ponies from Norway and Sweden, and East Russia and
Poland and Finland; the riding and driving horses
from Hanover and Hungary. Some, as we have seen,
come from the United States, some from Canada—the
Canadian horse having many admirers—and even the
South American mustang and the South Russian tarpan
have figured in the carriages with less than four
wheels licensed by the Board of Inland Revenue.

It is the general opinion that our carriage horses
are not as good as they used to be, and we are told
of the wonderful work that was accomplished by them
before the railway monopolised the long-distance passenger traffic. A carriage horse that travels a hundred
miles a week is now thought to be a treasure, but
many horses in the past did fifty miles a day. The
travelling carriage with its two horses would then do
about ten miles at the rate of six or seven miles an
hour, and halt for a quarter of an hour, during which
the horses would wash out their mouths and eat a wisp
of hay; the next stage would be about six miles, when
there would be a halt for half an hour, during which
the horses would be unharnessed and rubbed well down
and fed with half a peck of corn; at the end of another
ten miles there would be a halt of a quarter of an
hour and a bait as before; at the end of six miles further
there would be a halt of two hours, during which the
horses would have both hay and corn; then would
come another ten-mile stage, ending with a quarter of

an hour's bait; and then would come the remaining eight miles, at the end of which the horses would have a mash before their night meal. This was the way people travelled when George the Fourth was King, or perhaps it would be more correct to say, 'the way some people travelled,' for it is clear enough that this sort of horse was the exception and not the rule. Of course, a large number went by post-horses; and then there was the coach traffic, so curiously limited in its capacity.

There are coaches now; even during the winter there are half-a-dozen working on the roads to and from London; but these coaches can hardly be taken seriously as representing the coach of those 'glorious old days,' the recollection of which has lasted so much longer than their existence.

The mails have been carried by train for a longer period than they were carried by coach. The first mail coach appeared in August 1784, it having been then introduced by Major Palmer, the Duke of Richmond's son-in-law. What may be called the dominant idea of his invention was the cutting up of the road into short stages so as to change horses every ten miles, and use just as many horses as there were miles to be travelled. About 1835, when coaching was in its prime, there were seven hundred coaches at work, and these averaged ten miles an hour. Each horse ran for only one hour in the twenty-four, and stayed at home on the fourth day. He lasted about four years, and he cost 25l. to buy; but the horses used within the ten-mile radius of the large towns were very different from the roughish cattle that took their places along the country stretches. Nowadays our coaches are horsed with teams of level excellence all the way down. To horse the Brighton coach of 1891 forty-five horses were used, and these at Aldridge's realised under the hammer 3,811 guineas, or an average of 85 guineas each. In 1877 the Brighton stud fetched 80*l*. each ; in 1878 they fetched 75*l*. ; in 1885 the Guildford horses fetched 74*l*. 10*s*. each, and next year the Windsor horses fetched over 60*l*. The truth is that our modern coach-horses are really hunters, while the business coach-horse of the past was more of an omnibus horse. Of course the only coach-horses that come into our London 'world' are those used on the home stage, and their number is insignificant in a herd of hundreds of thousands such as that with which we are dealing.

As with the horses so with the coach. The present coach is merely a drag for passengers only, and differs greatly from the old mail, which went swinging along, with a lurch every now and then, no matter how cleverly it might be ballasted. Its fore boot was full of parcels, so was its hind boot; its roof was piled up with baggage, with a tarpaulin lashed over the pile ; game and baskets were hung on to its lamp irons ; and underneath it was a 'cradle' of more luggage, all carefully packed, it is true, but giving a very different look to the whole affair than we get to-day in the hand-some drags that leave the Métropole. The coaches, as now, were mostly supplied by contract. Vidler of Mill-bank was the great man, and he used to sell them right out at 140 guineas, or lend them out at so much a mile. And the horses were also hired out. Chaplin was the largest contractor ; he had 1,700 horses at one time at work on the roads out of London. Horne was another

contractor in an expansive way ; he, like Chaplin, had
been a driver, and the time came when he became his
partner, and dropping coaching took to cartage, for
which, as Chaplin and Horne, they became better
known.

As London now has its Cart-horse Parade, it had
then its parade of mail coaches, which took place at
Millbank, where the coaches were mostly built and the
harness made. It was held on May Day, and brought
together all the large London coach proprietors, the
Sherborns, the Hearnes, the Faggs, and others, men
who prided themselves on the fact that nowhere in the
world were to be found such horses, such coaches, such
drivers, or such guards. ' The coaches and harness were
either new or newly painted and furnished,' says Mr.
J. K. Fowler in his interesting *Echoes of Old Country
Life*, ' the horses in the pink of condition and beauty,
the coachmen and guards in new liveries of scarlet and
gold, each proprietor vieing with his opponent in an
endeavour to produce the most perfect turn-out. Critics
abounded, and the judges gave the awards unbiassed
by any predilections for the teams which passed through
their respective districts. The procession started, and
dense crowds of spectators thronged the route from
Westminster, through the Strand, Fleet Street, and
Ludgate Hill, by the Old Bailey, to the General Post
Office.'

The London proprietors did well at this coaching ;
the country ones did not. ' The London firms,' says
Mr. Fowler, ' had many great advantages over us.
Every coach that left any booking-office was charged
1*l*. per month for booking passengers, and as many

hundred coaches ran into London at 12*l*. per annum each, it became a very large sum for the Londoners to pocket, amounting to some thousands a year. Each coach was charged 12*s*. 6*d*. a week for washing and greasing the wheels; for every parcel or passenger twopence had to be paid for booking; the coachmen paid their takings into the London end, and thus the London proprietors had always thousands at their bankers. The accounts were made up monthly, and divided at so much per mile for their earnings, and each man who horsed the coach had his mileage sent him, whilst if any loss of parcels or otherwise had happened on his section of the road, he was the person made responsible. At every stage the coachman took what was called his way-bill into the office, and entered the number of passengers taken up and carried; their fares were placed in the proper column, and the money was given up at the journey's end. The proprietors were thus entirely at the mercy of the coachmen and guards, as there was no check upon the number of miles the passengers were recorded as having travelled. It was always considered that the Government, in duty and taxes, owned one wheel of the coach, and the coachman and guard purloined another wheel; the turnpikes, farriers, harnessmakers and coach-painters had another, which left one wheel only to the proprietors as their share of the profit.'

In the coaching heyday Hounslow was to London what Clapham Junction is now. 'A coach,' we are told, 'went through Hounslow every twelve minutes during the twenty-four hours!' Prodigious! One hundred and twenty coaches, carrying perhaps a dozen people each ! What would the good folk of Hounslow have thought of the six hundred trains that now go through Clapham in the same time ? What would our streets be like if we were to turn on to them all the people that now go by rail ? We should have the Hounslow road all the year round like Balham Hill on the Derby Day.

CHAPTER IX

THE JOBMASTER'S HORSE

IT takes over 300,000 living horse-power to move the wheels along the roads of London; and if we were to stand the horses in single file they would reach along the bridle-ways from St. Paul's to John-o'-Groat's.

In 1891 the City took its day census, and found that 92,372 vehicles entered that favoured square mile during twenty-four hours; of these a third, chiefly omnibuses and cabs, were probably counted more than once; but allowing for these we should still have over a hundred thousand horses crossing the City boundary inwards during a day.

Fired by the example of the City Fathers, the writer also took a census in a small way in perhaps not a particularly praiseworthy endeavour to discover how many horses came home from the Derby. Here was the horse-world of London boldly displayed—more, it must be confessed, to the advantage of the horses than to that of their drivers or freights. From the heavy dray horse to the coster's pony every variety of breed and quality was represented, including a solitary specimen of that favoured class which we are frequently assured is, in a fine spirit of philanthropy, only kept

H

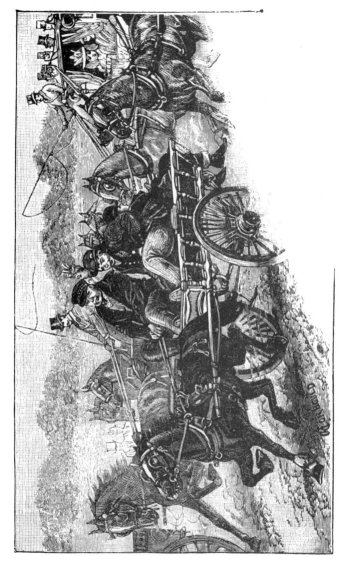

DERBY DAY

alive for the benefit of the race, and performs its useful function of leavening the mass much as does primogeniture. But London has no racehorses now, except they be merely passing through it. Even in the outer circle the old gate-money gatherings are dead, killed by a leisurely Jockey Club, which insisted on all such meetings being advertised in the *Racing Calendar*, and accepting no advertisements unless of meetings at which more than 300*l.* a day is given in 'added money'; and so the racehorse of the town, that used to go forth as a betting machine from an obscure London stable, passed out of existence, and his nearest representative is the Whitechapel trotter, which may occasionally be seen careering along the road on Sundays, to the no small danger of every one who is not top-heavy with intoxicants. And one of the noteworthy features of the return from the Derby is this peculiar safety of the drunken man, who, either on foot or on wheels, never seems to come to grief among the crowd. This crowd is a sight to see; but it fills the heart of the serious on-looker with sadness. Whatever else horse-racing may do, it certainly attracts an endless number of the vicious and the drunken, and it is a fair inference that it helps to make those who frequent it vicious and drunken. It is notorious that honesty and horse-racing seldom dwell together, and the spectacle of the Derby crowd on its return is an object lesson in the debasing power of what is miscalled sport.

And a miscellaneous collection of horses it exhibits. Here are horses from every county in Britain; horses from almost every country of Europe, and certainly a

few from Argentina; some from Canada; and at least
one from distant Australia, the horsiest continent in the
world, where every inhabitant has half a horse, whilst
in London county it takes fourteen to share a horse
amongst them.   How many they seem as they go past,
and yet how few they are compared with those that
stay at home!   The London streets are apparently as
full of horses on the Derby Day as on any day in the
year, and show no sign of the very slight weeding that
has gone to Epsom.   And a mere weeding it is, and
certainly has been for the last twenty years, although
the number of horses on the Epsom road on that day
is as great as it was twenty years ago.   We hear of
thousands, tens of thousands, even a hundred thousand
horses on the Downs, whereas as a matter of fact there
never was a tenth of the London horses gathered together at Epsom on the great Wednesday of the year.
Coming home the crowd is thickest up through Balham and along Clapham Common; and on that road,
notwithstanding all the fuss, there passed last year,
between five o'clock and nine o'clock, just 4,002 horses,
drawing or carrying about 50 short of 20,000 people;
so that there were five persons per horse, and a thousand
horses per hour.

Of these horses we shall be safe in saying that at
least nine-tenths of the good ones came from the jobmaster.   The 'master' is everywhere in the London
horse-world; even the butcher's cart and pony are getting to be hired, and it says so on some of the shafts.
A large number of costers have hired from what we
suppose they would call 'time immemorial.'   The hire
system pervades everything; we have even in our

foragings discovered a happy man with a stock of 5,000 hand-barrows, which he lets out at three-halfpence an hour.

Some of the 'masters' do an enormous business, the one in the largest way being apparently Tilling of Peckham, who has a stud of 2,500 horses; and an interesting business it is, owing to its wide extent and many developments.   There are Tilling's horses on the job as far north as Sunderland on the Tees; westwards you will find them in Cornwall; southwards you will get them at Brighton.   Horses he has of all varieties, from the heavy cart horse to the handy cob; but not of all qualities, for it does not pay a jobmaster to have a bad-looking horse, advertisement, if not noblesse, obliging.   Tilling jobs for the duke, the doctor, and the drayman; for all sorts and conditions, from the Lord Mayor and Sheriffs to the washerwoman limited.   Besides those in his own omnibuses and cabs, he has one batch of horses in the carts of a London district Board of Works; another, of 100, he has in Peek Frean's biscuit vans; another he has in the bottled-beer vans of one of the 'princely' brewers.   He horses a tram line in the east; he horses another tram line in the south. He horses the Fire Brigade, the Salvage Corps, and, quite recently, he has begun to horse the Police.   To do all this requires a large establishment, with yards open night and day, an establishment in which a rise in corn meant an increase of 9,000*l.* in the forage bill of one year only.

The best horses are, of course, those used for fashionable carriage work.   The high-class harness horse comes to London when he is about four years old.

He is untrained, undrilled, with all his troubles to be faced. The young cart-horse is gradually introduced to work on the farm ; not so the carriage horse, who is too much of the possibility of a valuable animal to run any risks with. He may fetch 80*l.* ; but if he is a handsome, well-built, upstanding state-coach horse, of the kind now so much sought after, he will be cheap at 120*l.* He has to be educated to behave himself like a gentleman ; he must learn to stand well—not an easy thing to do—he must know how to back and turn gracefully, how to draw up stylishly at a front door, how to look nice when under window criticism, how to carry his head and lift his feet, and how to work with a companion and be as like him in action as one pea is like another ; in short, he has to go through a complete course of deportment, though not of dancing, and he will be a promising pupil if he gets through it in eight months. If he does well and shows a willing mind, it is well with him and he has an easy time of it for years ; but if he is tricky or perverse in any way he may have to go to hard labour and spend a twelvemonth in a 'bus. Sometimes that breaks him thoroughly of his bad habits and he returns to carriage work; sometimes, like an habitual criminal, he refuses to amend, and he remains a 'bus horse for life. And herein is the advantage of a miscellaneous business, for if a horse will not do in one branch he may in another.

The new horse is not branded or numbered, but a note is made of his marks, and he is named from a book of names, taking, perhaps, an old name which has been vacant for at least a year ; the names being chosen as fitting the particular horse, and not as aiding the memory with regard to the date or circumstance of his purchase, naming from pedigree, as in the case of a racer, being, of course, out of the question. There are many systems of naming; some firms, like Truman & Hanbury, and Spiers & Pond, give the horses names which begin with the same initial all through the year, so that the A's may show the horses bought in 1890, the B's those bought in 1891, the C's those bought in 1892, &c.; others have other plans, but nothing of this systematic sort seems to exist in the livery trade, owing, perhaps, to the possibility of awkward developments in the event of the customer learning the key.

When the horse has passed his drills and been pronounced efficient, he takes his place with eight or nine others in a stable which has its roof thatched inside, so as to keep the temperature equable in summer and winter; and in every one of these stables the horses are as much as possible of the same colour and size, so as to look their best amid their comfortable surroundings. There are fixed travises and no bales for this class of horse, and no peat, but the usual straw, both for the sake of appearance and to save his coat from roughening. He is as well cared for as the plate at a silversmith's, and, like it, is not often so well treated when out on hire. But horses of all grades are nowadays better treated than they used to be, even though there may be deterioration in their quality, which, to say the least of it, is doubtful.

The past is always better than the present with both horse and man, for memory and imagination play strange tricks with judgment. Like the artist, they make their picture by selection, rejection, and composition. Even with the living horse, how much his beauties increase as his distance from us increases! The ease with which a man will lose his eye for a horse is notorious. Let even a good judge live for awhile among second-class horses, and he will insensibly modify his ideal; and he will only get back to his true taste by another stay in first-class company. Hearsay and recollection are simply misleading; and if this is the case with the living horse, what are we to say of his grandfathers? The only true test of a horse is to bring him into daylight and place him between two samples of the class to which he claims to belong. Look at him there; pick out the differences in every limb and feature; if he stands that test he need fear no other. And as the horse of the past cannot be brought to the scratch in this way, there is safety in enlarging on his merits, though some of us will be content to listen in the same attitude of philosophic doubt with which we would listen to the description of a living horse at third or fourth hand. The horse of the past had his particular work, the horse of the present has his, and is probably better suited for it than his ancestor would be, just as the horse of the future will probably be better adapted for whatever may be the particular work he is specially bred for.

The state-carriage horse is bred for show, and there is a good deal of truth in the statement that he is as fondly watched as a mother's darling. He must not travel more than fourteen miles a day, for if he did he would spoil his action; he must not be out all the week round, for that would spoil his coat; he must be kept to town work, for in the country his graces would be

lost ; and he must keep as much as possible to the level,
or he would not stand nicely on his legs. If you want
to climb hills you must have a shorter-legged horse—
in fact, if you want use you must have a useful animal ;
and the sum of the matter is that you must take your
dealer or jobmaster into your confidence and tell him
exactly what you want, and he will fit you with a horse
much as a tailor will find you a ready-made coat.

This point is curiously brought out amongst the
doctors. The man with a consulting practice wants
a different sort of horse to the humbler general practitioner. The consulting man must have a pair that
go fast and well, and cover long distances, and draw up
at the door in a style that will inspire the patient and
the patient's friends with faith—and move the G.P. to
envy. The said G.P. must have a horse that is ready
for work at all hours, and looks none the worse for
standing about in the rain ; in other words, one wants
a coach-horse, and other wants a good hackney, which
some would consider the better horse of the two.

Most of the doctors are horsed by the jobmaster.
Some of the Harley Street and Cavendish Square men
have half-a-dozen horses on hire, which means a nice
little addition to their expenses. The horses are usually
foraged by the jobmaster, and every fortnight the feed
is delivered in sacks at the stable ; but the shoeing is
done by a local farrier, though at the jobmaster's
expense.

There is no doubt that the typical doctor's horse,
the horse of the hard-working general practitioner, has
a trying life. Like the maid-of-all-work, his work is

never done; and he must be exceptionally sound and robust to stand the wear and tear of day and night, particularly on what we may call the outer edge of London. He may not look so well as the animal driven by the country medico, who generally takes a pride in his horseflesh, but he costs quite as much and does not last as long. Six years' work is as much as can be expected of him, and the expectation is frequently unfulfilled, for as a rule he has little time to be comfortable either in the stable or the street, although many a one-horse doctor walks his round on Sunday, to give his weary steed a rest. Of late years influenza has been exceptionally hard on the doctor's horse; it has hit him in two ways: as an ailment from which he suffers, and as a cause of much extra work. No wonder that the doctor jobs, and avails himself of an inexhaustible supply of horse power, in which the risk is spread over thousands instead of being concentrated on his one poor pill-box bay.

The daily round of the doctor's horse must be as monotonous as that of the milkman's. As a contrast we have the festive outings of that holiday animal, the wedding grey. As we have before noticed, the grey horse is not appreciated by the cabman, nor is he much loved by the omnibus owner or the carrier, but the livery stableman cannot do without him. For a wedding he is indispensable, though in a crush of weddings chestnuts have to take his place, just as in a crush of funerals the 'black masters' have to call on their brethren for the loan of darkish bays and browns.

Tilling averages half-a-dozen weddings a day all the

OUT FOR A HOLIDAY

year round, Sundays excepted, for Sunday is not a
favourite marriage day among the folks who patronise
the jobmaster. To horse these weddings takes about
forty horses, most of which do nothing else; but taking
London round, the wedding horse is a superior kind of
'bus horse out for a holiday, which he owes not to his
merits and points, but to his colour; and it has been
observed that the melancholy air with which he eyes
the bride and bridegroom is due not so much to his
forebodings as to their future, but to his veiling his joy
at having such a light day's work.

Very different is it with the fire-engine horse, which
comes prancing forth so vigorously from sheer delight
at getting out into fresh air. Our fire brigade, efficient
as it may be, is not as other brigades. If you touch
the button of a fire-alarm in Toronto, every gong in
every station, and every bell in every church tower, will
strike the number of the particular button you have
pushed. Every alarm post in the streets is numbered.
Say you touch No. 24. Instantly, clang, clang go the
bells for the tens, and then pause, and go again, clang,
clang, clang, clang for the units, and everyone knows
there is a fire in the district in which No. 24 post is
situated. And as the bells begin to clang, the people
passing the doors of the station instinctively spring
aside, for before the clanging is over the doors fly open
outwards, and the engine is already on the move.
Where Europe counts minutes, America counts seconds.
Our need may not be as urgent, but surely, like a penny,
a second saved is a second to the good, particularly in
the case of a fire.

Our system of horsing fire-engines is a survival from the time when the brigade requisitioned any passing horses for the purpose of dragging the engine. The American fire-engine horse is the property of the brigade ; ours is the property of the jobmaster, who not only feeds him and looks after him, but lends the harness ; and this last is the answer to the question so frequently heard at a fire, ' Why does the brigade have L.C.C. on its engines and T.T. on its blinkers ? '

Tilling has sixty horses in the fire-engines : the other seventy are supplied by other jobmasters in different parts of London. Hence the difference in the quality of the engine-horses, and the varying rates at which they travel. Even in the harness they are not quite alike, and few of the elaborate automatic arrangements of the Americans are in use. But in the working of these arrangements the American horse has to undergo a year's training, while our horse is fit for its simple work in three months. Theirs costs 60*l*., ours does not cost as much ; and theirs lasts but three and a half years, while ours lasts eight.

The American fire horse requires almost as much training as a circus performer. In his harnessing only two things are not automatic, these being his rush from the stall to the pole, and the snapping of the collar over his head. The instant the electric circuit opens to send the alarm, the current drops a metal ball alongside the gong, which, as it strikes, presses down a brass bar and pulls a steel wire that automatically unhitches the springs ; and when the driver grasps the reins, the tension looses the spring, the harness drops on the horses, the watchman grasps the collar, and the weights in the ceiling carry up the hangers clear of everything as the horses rush out of the open door.

But how, it may be asked, does the driver happen to be in his place? The answer is that the men sleep on the first floor, close to a trap which is surrounded by a brass railing. At the first stroke of the gong they spring from their beds, seize the railing, and let themselves drop through the trap, seizing a second bar as they do so, and steadying themselves on to their seats in time to receive the horses which have left their mangers at the fall of the ball. To train a horse to play his part in a pantomimic performance of this kind is a serious task, but that it is accomplished is a sufficient answer to the objector, and it is simple folly to deny the saving of time which is notorious to everyone who has crossed the Atlantic. In short, our drill is smart to those who have not seen smarter, although we get through our work with far fewer failures and much less fuss.

Grey being a conspicuous colour, the grey horse is apparently more fortunate than others in getting a clear road, and he does well in an engine. But although the engine-horse is rarely troubled with burns, and is quite heedless of the sparks which sprinkle on to his back from the unguarded funnel, he is not free from other accidents; and the contractor has to replace him by night or day on receipt of a telephone message from the fire station, so that horses have always to be held in readiness at the yard for emergencies.

All the large horse-owners have infirmaries to which the sick and injured are sent, and most of them have a farm for the convalescent. Tilling's infirmary is a special yard about a quarter of a mile from headquarters, where there are over sixty loose boxes and stalls for the patients under treatment. We have already seen how curiously alike to man the horse is in his ailments. This is all the more noticeable at this infirmary from the fact of a slate appearing on each door, on which is written the patient's name, his complaint, and the treatment ordered; it only wants a blue paper by the side of it, to be sent to the dispenser for the medicine, to make the resemblance to a hospital complete.

The horses that die in a livery stable are few, but those cleared out every year amount to about 12 per cent. This gives an average of eight and a half years' work, but it is spread over so many kinds of horses as to be hardly worth consideration.

We have already spoken at length of the vestry dray horse. One thing, however, we did not mention about him, and that is that he has the biggest starting pull of any horse in London when he is in the shafts of a water-cart. The cart weighs a ton and three quarters, and there are two and a quarter tons of water in the tank, so that he has to drag up four tons from the channels to the crown of the road, often a short but not an easy gradient. It is owing to this tremendous pull that, according to Mr. Stanley, he goes wrong so quickly in his forelegs; and to save this, that well-known veterinary surgeon proposes to lift the pitching in front of the hydrants just enough to give the struggling horse a fair start with the loaded van—a trifling change that would probably add months to the horse's life.

Of the lighter cart horse, familiarly known as the ' vanner,' and costing about 55*l.*, we may have something to say later on. The value of the coach and carriage horses we arrived at in our last chapter. Taking London through, the fire-engine horse is of the ' artillery' brand, much like the police horse, and is probably worth 40*l.*   At 5*l.* less than that we can put the 'bus horses, at 5*l.* less than that the cab horses, and within the next 5*l.* we should certainly have the horses jobbed in the tradesmen's carts.   These are not, perhaps, the prices that would be realised under the hammer; but the value of horses can hardly be taken at repository rates.

CHAPTER X

THE COAL HORSE

On the average every Londoner burns a quarter of a pound of coal an hour. This may not seem to be much, and at first sight one would think that the various societies for smoke-abatement and so-called fog abolition had very poor grounds for their existence; but a quarter of a pound of coal an hour means six pounds of coal a day, and that means a ton of coal a year; so that London annually burns five million tons. If we add these five millions to the close upon three millions used by the gas companies, we get the close upon eight millions which are now entering the London area during the year by land or water.

There are not many horses used in shifting the gas coal, but nearly all the five millions used outside the gas manufacture is moved from wharf and railway station by hiring horse-power. The number of horses employed in this work is great, though not so great as might perhaps be imagined. The coal horse—that is the first-class coal-merchant's horse, such as works the vans of Herbert Clarke, for instance—moves about thirty tons a week, or 1,500 tons in the course of the year. If all the horses were like these, and the coal had to be moved but once, as is generally the case, it would require over 3,000 horses in the London coal trade. As a matter of fact, there are about five thousand more, but these run down to a very decided fag end of greengrocers' drudges and cab-yard screws, which we can conveniently eliminate.

There are 300 horses working out of the Great Northern King's Cross depôt alone; the Midland and North Western have almost as many, and all the railway coal stations are tended by a numerous herd of distributors, so that we shall be well within the mark in allotting 1,500 fairly good horses to the leading London coal merchants. The average of the inner ring of the trade is about a hundred horses each. This may not seem much, but a hundred horses at 55*l*. apiece means 5,500*l*., a nice little capital to have to invest in horseflesh alone.

The better-class coal horse is of the heavy dray horse type, and comes to London when he is five years old, either from the fair or direct from the farm. He costs from 50*l*. to 70*l*., and he averages from three to eight years of hard work. When he begins to fail he is sold to what we may call the second-class merchants for an average of 20*l*.; or he may be worked on, and he very often is, until he finds his way to the repository, and changes hands at 10*l*., to be put to miscellaneous labour. It is the same story with these horses as with all the rest. Some will only last a couple of years, some will go on for ten or twelve, and there is one horse at least in the London carts who in his time has drawn 18,000 tons of coal, and looks fit to draw quite half as many more.

THE COAL HORSE

The coal horse breakfasts at four in the morning and goes out to work at six, taking with him a nose-bag and a small sack of bait, which is his provender for the day. He does not return to the stables until his day's work is done, which may end at seven o'clock or may last out till eleven. He may do two long journeys, or perhaps as many as four short ones ; any way, his average runs out at the thirty tons, two tons going to each load. Now that the coal merchant, unlike the grocer, is not allowed to weigh in the bag, the van, the weighing machine, the weights and sacks and sundries, amount to rather over a ton, so that a full load means not less than three tons, which has often to be taken long distances, although compensation comes in by the horse having to stand about a good deal while loading and delivering. This load is taken on the level and up easy gradients, and a horse will be driven a long way round to avoid a hill; but when the hill has to be faced the journeys are arranged so that two vans will climb the hill together, one being left in the valley while the horse is harnessed on, tandem fashion, to the other van to haul it up, both horses returning for the other van. In this way most of the London hills are negotiated ; but there is at least one hill, Hollybush Hill, out Highgate way, where the coal carts go up behind an improvised team of three.

Six days a week does the coal horse work, averaging, with due allowance for Saturdays, eighty hours, thirty of them in front of three tons, thirty in front of one and a half, and twenty standing at ease. On Sunday he has a whole day's rest, and very glad he is to get it.

He is gradually eased in to his work. At first he

A COMPENSATING REST

is out but three days a week; then he gets four, then five, then six; and after a little experience on London's varied pavings and gradings he may come to be set one of his most difficult tasks, that of dragging a load along St. John Street Road, uphill, on the way from the Meat Market to the Angel. If he can stand that slippery track he can stand anything. On it the granite squares are so wide as just to have their corners rounded off by wear, and they lie like petrified puddings on which no shoe can get a grip. These big granite pitchings are the abhorred of coal drivers; what they like is the more general three inches by six with which the railway companies pave their yards, a size that wears as much at the edges as the corners, and is just wide enough to give a satisfactory foothold.

The really good coal horse is much like 'the horse that walks' of the railway companies. 'What we want,' said a horse-keeper to us, 'is a stout bit of timber like this'—and he stroked the near hind cannon approvingly —' and a good pair of breeches'—and he smacked the quarter—' and a biggish tub'—and his hand travelled down the girth—' not too long, you know! and an arm like that'— and he touched it with two fingers—' and a shoulder! ah!'—and he looked at it admiringly— ' steady, boy, steady!'—and he looked again—' and a neck— well, there!' That is it exactly. There! We need say no more. The horse was a black, said to be five years old, standing about sixteen hands, and weighing about as many hundredweight.

Some of these horses are shires, some of them Clydesdales, some of them would more than satisfy the Leicestershire people as not being eligible for entry in

any stud-book. You can see them of all sorts, good,
bad, and indifferent, at work in dozens up that curious
thoroughfare—though it looks like a *cul-de-sac*—which
runs out of Pancras Road under the arches by Battle
Bridge, round by the gasworks and between the Midland and Great Northern Railways. There you will
find coals to the left of you, coals to the right of you,
volleying and thundering. In every arch is a platform ;
on every platform are two weighing machines ; over
each weighing machine is a shoot which delivers into
the sacks on the scales, and from which the coal stream
is cut off with a lever much as you turn off your water
at a tap. Overhead are the waggons ; down the shoots
the coal roars, and booms, and hisses in a cloud of dust,
as sack after sack fills up and is run out on the hand
truck into the vans, in the shafts of which stand the
horses gently bobbing their nosebags and utterly indifferent to the dust and din. And if you are observant
you will notice that the initials on the harness do not
always correspond to the staring name on the carts,
thereby showing that the horses are jobbed, or that the
firm has an *alias* ; and some of these firms have as many
names as a princess of the very Highest Mightiness.

Most of the horses are fairly good, for it requires a
fairly good horse to drag the weight. Some of them
are occasionally in the first flight in the Cart-horse
Parade, a show which might do more for the quality of
London horses if, in addition to its present prizes, it
were to give some for the best horses that have been
five years, or even more, in one employ. The best
horse and the best looked after is the one that lasts
longest and works best at middle age. To encourage

the 'coalies' to take care of their horses, a gratuity is
generally given at Christmas time to those who have
done best in this way, a reward which is, however,
frequently earned more by luck than judgment.

The coal horse meets with the same accidents as
the rest of the heavy brigade; he is run into, and he
picks up nails, and has his feet run over, and so on.
And he has the sores from his collar and harness in wet
weather, and all the other ailments we have met with
in so many of his brethren. When he loses form, he is
often cleared out, as we have said, to masters in a
smaller way of business, men who have more of one-ton
work, or have easy roads in suburban neighbourhoods,
or simply work their horseflesh on the cheap.

The coal trade is managed a good deal on the
branch system. The large merchants have ten or a
dozen small studs of horses out in different parts of
London, near the larger local railway stations from
which the coal is obtained for retail distribution. In
these stables there are from five to twenty horses—ten
is the average—and in all respects they are worked like
the central depôts to which the horses are first attached,
and from which they usually get their feed. Very few
of these stables are on two floors, nearly all being on
the ground; as a rule they are particularly roomy and
airy, with no fixed travises, but the common double
bale; generally with straw litter, though occasionally
with peat, and the resulting difficulty as to the disposal
of the waste—capital examples, in fact, of a cart-horse
stable in which a few horses are kept under the best of
conditions for health and efficiency. Here and there,
among the second-rate men, the old dark stuffy den is

the horse's home; but, as we have already said, the average horse is treated much better than he used to be; he is better fed, better housed, and more intelligently looked after, and he lives longer, works more, and is better worth looking at than in the merry days of the past.

A SAMPLE OF THE BLACK BRIGADE

CHAPTER XI

THE BLACK BRIGADE

A GOOD many of the coal horses are blacks and dark bays, and by some people they are known as 'the black brigade'; but the real black brigade of London's trade are the horses used for funerals. This funeral business is a strange one in many respects, but, just as the job-master is in the background of the every-day working world, so the jobmaster is at the back of the burying world. The 'funeral furnisher' is equal to all emergencies on account of the facilities he possesses for hiring to an almost unlimited extent, so long as the death rate is normal. The wholesale men, the 'black masters,' are always ready to cope with a rate of twenty per thousand —London's normal is seventeen—but when it rises above that, as it did in the influenza time, the pressure is so great that the 'blacks' have to get help from the 'coloured,' and the 'horse of pleasure' becomes familiar with the cemetery roads.

A hundred years ago there was but one black master in London. He owned all the horses; and there are wonderful stories of the funerals in those days when railways were unknown. The burying of a duke or even a country squire, in the family vault, was then a serious matter, for the body had to be taken the whole distance by road, and the horses were sometimes away for a week or more, and were often worked in relays, much on the same plan as the coach-horses, only that rapid progress through the towns and villages was impossible, for the same reason that no living undertaker dare trot with a tradesman within the limits of the district in which the deceased happens to have been known and respected. Even nowadays the black masters of London can be counted on one's fingers, the chief, according to general report, being Dottridge, of East Road.

A wonderful place is Dottridge's. It is the centre of what may be called the wholesale undertaking trade, where the retail undertakers are themselves undertaken and supplied with all they need, from coffin to tombstone. From all parts of the country telegrams and letters are continually coming in and packages continually going out by carrier and fast train, all labelled ' immediately for funeral,' to insure quick delivery. If anyone wants a parcel to go promptly and surely to hand, he has only to label it with these mystic words, and the railway men will pounce upon it and be off with it at a run—that is, if they treat it as we saw them do with the first one that came under our notice, which they handled as if it had arrived red hot, and was required at its destination before it cooled. 'Haste,' ' urgent,' ' immediate,' are but poor incentives to speed compared with the red funeral label, such as was once accidentally stuck on a boy's hamper, and sent the matron into hysterics as it was hurriedly bumped on to the school door-mat.

Hundreds of men are at work. Here is a wood yard, such as one is accustomed to see by a canal side. Here are 'caskets' of every size and pattern being made by steam machinery, sawing machines, planing machines, fretting machines, bending machines, sand-papering machines, all in full swing; besides a complete outfit for marble working and carving, another for brass working, and, to say nothing of the carriage repairing and harness making, a battery-room for electro-plating. If anyone wants a shudder, let him take a peep at the sample room and the stores below, in which are those terrible boxes of one shape but all kinds—brass, lead, wood, paper, wickerwork, the last recommended as ' looking well when covered with green moss and flowers '; you can try one on if you like, as you would an overcoat, and see if it fits. There they are in dozens, of all qualities, from the panelled and carved down to the simplest, plain, unpolished, undecorated shell in which every Jew, from the millionaire to the sweated Pole, goes to his grave—for Dottridge's have for years held the contract of burying all the Jews of London.

These funeral things—funereal does not quite give the meaning—are ordered, not in ordinary language, but by code, as foreign telegrams are worked, some trivial word doing duty for perhaps a full page of descriptive matter. A telegram will come in at nine o'clock with, perhaps, merely a word in it, say Malachite —or whatever it may be—and in reply there will be at Euston, or St. Pancras, or Paddington, ready for the twelve o'clock train, a long flat package of six boards, which the country or suburban undertaker will put together like a puzzle. He wires for ' the wood,' and the wood comes to him all ready for 'building,' drapery, furniture, and all complete, the plate to follow within an hour or two of the receipt of the inscription, the quickest thing of all being the silver-plating, for no plated goods are stocked, and the brass is invariably plated, polished, and despatched on the day the order is received.

Dottridge's are ' at the back ' of all the big funerals in London. They buried Mr. Spurgeon ; they buried Mrs. Booth ; years ago they buried Cardinal Wiseman, the biggest 'black horse job' ever known, for the Roman Catholics will always have black horses if they can get them. Mr. Spurgeon had coloured horses, so had Mrs. Booth, but when Cardinal Manning died, the priests crowded to the East Road for coaches to follow, and were much disconcerted to find there were not enough blacks to horse them.

Altogether there are about 700 of these black horses in London. They are all Flemish, and come to us from the flats of Holland and Belgium by way of Rotterdam and Harwich. They are the youngest horses we import, for they reach us when they are rising three years old, and take a year or so before they get into full swing ; in fact, they begin work as what we may call the ' half-timers ' of the London horse-world. When young they cost rather under than over a hundred guineas a pair, but sometimes they get astray among the carriage folk, who pay for them, by mistake of course, about double the money. In about a year or more, when they have got over their sea-sickness and other ailments, and have been trained and acclimatised, they fetch 65*l.* each ; if they do not turn out quite good enough for first-class work they are cleared out to the second-class men at about twenty-five guineas; if they go to the repository they average 10*l*. ; if they go to the knacker's they average thirty-five shillings, and they generally go there after six years' work. Most of them are stallions, for Flemish geldings go shabby and brown. They are cheaper now than they were a year or two back, for the ubiquitous American took to buying them in their native land for importation to the States, and thereby sent up the price; but the law of supply and demand came in to check the rise, and some enterprising individual actually took to importing black horses here from the States, and so spoilt the corner.

Here, in the East Road, are about eighty genuine Flemings, housed in capital stables, well built, lofty, light, and well ventilated, all on the ground floor. Over every horse is his name, every horse being named from the celebrity, ancient or modern, most talked about at the time of his purchase, a system which has a somewhat comical side when the horses come to be worked together. Some curious traits of character are revealed among these celebrities as we pay our call at their several stalls. General Booth, for instance, is 'most amiable, and will work with any horse in the stud'; all the Salvationists 'are doing well,' except Railton, 'who is showing too much blood and fire. Last week he had a plume put on his head for the first time, and that upset him.' Stead, according to his keeper, is 'a good horse, a capital horse—showy perhaps, but some people like the showy; he does a lot of work, and fancies he does more than he does. We are

trying him with General Booth, but he will soon tire
him out, as he has done others. He wouldn't work
with Huxley at any price!' Curiously enough, Huxley
' will not work with Tyndall, but gets on capitally with
Dr. Barnardo.' Tyndall, on the other hand, ' goes well
with Dickens,' but has a decided aversion to Henry
Ward Beecher. Morley works ' comfortably' with
Balfour, but Harcourt and Davitt ' won't do as a pair
anyhow.' An ideal team seems to consist of Bradlaugh,
John Knox, Dr. Adler, and Cardinal Manning. But
the practice of naming horses after church and chapel
dignitaries is being dropped owing to a superstition of
the stable. ' All the horses,' the horsekeeper says,
' named after that kind of person go wrong somehow !'
And so we leave Canon Farrar, and Canon Liddon, and
Dr. Punshon, and John Wesley and other lesser lights,
to glance at the empty stalls of Abraham, Isaac, and
Jacob, now ' out on a job,' and meet in turn with
Sequah and Pasteur, Mesmer and Mattei. Then we
find ourselves amid a bewildering mixture of poets,
politicians, artists, actors, and musicians.

' Why don't you sort them out into stables, and
have a poet stable, an artist stable, and so on ?'

' They never would stand quiet. The poets would
never agree ; and as to the politicians—well, you know
what politicians are, and these namesakes of theirs are
as like them as two peas !' And so the horses after
they are named have to be changed about until they
find fit companions, and then everything goes har-
moniously. The stud is worked in sections of four ;
every man has four horses which he looks after and
drives ; under him being another man, who drives

when the horses go out in pairs instead of in the team.

One would think these horses were big, black retriever dogs, to judge by the liking and understanding which spring up between them and their masters. It is astonishing what a lovable, intelligent animal a horse is when he finds he is understood. According to popular report these Flemish stallions are the most vicious and ill-tempered of brutes; but those who keep them and know them are of the very opposite opinion.

'I am not a horsey man,' said Mr. Dottridge to us, 'but I have known this one particular class of horse all my life, and I say they are quite affectionate and good-natured, and seem to know instinctively what you say to them and what you want. If you treat them well they will treat you well. One thing they have is an immense amount of self-esteem, and that you have to humour. Of course I have to choose the horses, and I do not choose the vicious ones. I can tell them by the peculiar glance they give as they look round at me. The whole manner of the horse, like the whole manner of a man, betrays his character. Even his nose will tell you. People make fun of Roman noses; now I never knew a horse with a Roman nose to be ill-natured. The horse must feel that your will is stronger than his, and he does feel it instinctively. He knows at once if a man is afraid of him or even nervous, and no man in that state will ever do any good with a horse. Even when you are driving, if you begin to get nervous, the horse knows it instantly. He is in communication with you by means of the rein, and he is somehow sensible of the change in your mind, although perhaps you are hardly conscious of it. I have no doubt whatever but that you can influence a horse even when he is ill, by mere power of will. There are affinities between man and horse which are at present inexplicable, but they exist all the same.'

There is an old joke about the costermonger's donkey who looked so miserable because he had been standing for a week between two hearse horses, and had not got over the depression. The reply to this is that the depression is mutual. The 'black family' has always to be alone; if a coloured horse is stood in one of the stalls, the rest of the horses in the stable will at once become miserable and fretful. The experiment has been tried over and over again, and always with the same result; and thus it has come about that in the black master's yards, the coloured horses used for ordinary draught work are always in a stable by themselves.

The funeral horse hardly needs description. The breed has been the same for centuries. He stands about sixteen hands, and weighs between 12 and 13 cwt. The weight behind him is not excessive, for the car does not weigh over 17 cwt., and even with a lead coffin he has the lightest load of any of our draught horses. The worst roads he travels are the hilly ones to Highgate, Finchley, and Norwood. These he knows well and does not appreciate. In a few months he gets to recognise all the cemetery roads 'like a book,' and after he is out of the bye streets he wants practically no driving, as he goes by himself, taking all the proper corners and making all the proper pauses. This knowledge of the road has its inconveniences, as it is often difficult to get him past the familiar corner when he is out at exercise. But of late he has had exercise enough at work, and during the influenza epidemic was doing his three and four trips a day, and the funerals had to take place not to suit the convenience of the relatives, but the available horse-power of the undertaker. Six days a week he works, for after a long agitation there are now no London funerals on Sundays, except perhaps those of the Jews, for which the horses have their day's rest in the week.

To feed such a horse costs perhaps two shillings a day—it is a trifle under that, over the 700—and his food differs from that of any other London horse. In his native Flanders he is fed a good deal upon slops, soups, mashes, and so forth; and as a Scotsman does best on his oatmeal, so the funeral horse, to keep in condition, must have the rye-bread of his youth. Rye-bread, oats, and hay form his mixture, with perhaps a little clover, but not much, for it would not do to heat him, and beans and such things are absolutely forbidden. Every Saturday he has a mash like other horses, but unlike them his mash consists, not of bran alone, but of bran and linseed in equal quantities. What the linseed is for we know not; it may be, as a Life Guardsman suggested to us, to make his hair glossy, that beautiful silky hair which is at once his pride and the reason of his special employment, and the sign of his delicate, sensitive constitution.

LIFE GUARDS

CHAPTER XII

THE CAVALRY HORSE

THERE is no more eloquent testimony to the orderliness of London than the mere sprinkling of cavalry within its limits. It may seem ridiculous to the foreigner that with 375 mounted police, and two small regiments of Household troops numbering 275 horses each, five millions of people are content to behave themselves; but it is a state of affairs of which Englishmen have no cause to be ashamed. Even adding in the six battalions of Foot Guards and the line battalion at the Tower, and considering that there is Woolwich, and that there are Hounslow and Windsor not far off, and that there are facilities of communication—not, however, greater than exist in other capitals—we shall find that the police, and military ready to be used as police, in and about London, are a mere handful compared to what are necessary for peace-keeping and ceremonial purposes in the cities across the Channel. And the display made of these is proportionately much less, for, as a matter of fact, the ordinary Londoner is aware of the presence of cavalry by reason only of the two specimens on view daily in Whitehall.

At one time the black horses of the Household

cavalry came almost entirely from Yorkshire and North Lincolnshire, most of them being expressly bred for the service. But of late we have changed all that. In those days the cavalry colonels had so much money allowed them for remounts, and they had to pick up their horses where they could, with the jobmaster at their elbow—for a consideration—to help them at a pinch ; and some of the London jobmasters had a standing order to be on the look-out for likely horses for certain regiments. Nowadays the Dublin dealer has taken the place of the London man, and, instead of the colonel buying horses, the buying is done by the Remount Department, whose happy hunting ground is Ireland.

When a military horse is 'cast,' and all military horses are 'cast' at fourteen years old, whether they be good, bad, or indifferent, a requisition for a substitute goes to the Remount Department at Woolwich, and the substitute arrives a day or two afterwards from the Emerald Isle, generally shipped direct by Daly or some other Dublin dealer. That the new horse is as good to look at as the old Yorkshire one, we have not heard any soldier declare, but he is at least thirty per cent. cheaper, and he seems to be strong enough for his work.

A British army corps, when discoverable, will be found to have 12,000 horses, of which 3,134 will be in the cavalry and 2,987 in the artillery; these 6,121 horses ought to be thoroughly broken and trained, even if the remainder are not. There are said to be only 70,000 horses in the British Isles fit for army work, but this is one of those pleasant fictions of which it is left to the foreigner to discover the fallacy. Like a good many other statements regarding our preparedness for self-defence, it is to be taken plus x, x representing the dominant number.

When Napoleon attempted to invade us—an attempt that was defeated at Trafalgar, which to the uninitiated may seem to be a long way off for the defeat of such a scheme, although any future attempt will probably have to be reckoned with still further at sea—the Government took stock of every horse in the kingdom, with the intention of a general impressment for military service; and nowadays the Government has power in times of national peril to lay hands on every horse within these islands, in preparation for which there are thousands of horses under subsidy with a view to immediate use. And when this seizure does take place, it will certainly not be to the joy of the jobmaster; he above all men shudders at the mere mention of foreign invasion, for invasion to him means the entire loss of his means of livelihood, and this at a sacrifice, for no Government would pay the price at which the jobmaster's stud has been collected.

The Life Guardsman's horse used to cost 60*l*., being the most expensive horse in the army; we shall not put him offensively cheap in these times at 20*l*. less; nor shall we be divulging any secrets of state in estimating that the cost of mounting the two regiments of cavalry in London—barring the officers' chargers—does not exceed 22,000*l*.

And yet the horses are carefully chosen and seem fit for their work, when either in or out of harness. They, of course, look their best at Knightsbridge, for at Knightsbridge the stabling is distinctly good, better even than is promised in the new barracks in Albany Street; but then a soldier's horse in stable generally looks better than a civilian's, owing to his head being where his tail should be. The civilian's horse always has his head over the manger; the soldier's horse is turned round as soon as he has finished his feed, and so gets more fresh air; the consequence of which admirable arrangement for preventing a horse ' breathing his own breath,' is that the visitor on entering the stable sees a double line of intelligent heads, instead of an avenue of hocks and tails.

Time was when every soldier's horse had a name, the initial of which was that of the troop to which he belonged. ' A ' troop had all A's, ' B ' had all B's, and so on; but in these days the squadron is the unit, not the troop, and the name has given place to the number. Every horse, then, has his number placed on a card over his manger, and the horses are separated from each other by a pole doing duty as a bale, and on each upright is the horse's kit, including the two spare shoes which every trooper carries, but not including the arms, which, of course, are kept elsewhere. This kit, and the arms and the rider, make up a nice little load, which averages out at twenty-three stone per man; not quite so heavy as that of our fat old knights, but still heavy enough for the class of horse which has nothing of the ' dray ' type about it.

It is not easy to get these horses of uniform type and character. There are many exchanges and rejections, and it often happens that a horse sent in for cavalry work has to go to the draught, to the Artillery, or even the Transport service; so that though the remainder may not be examples of the much-talked-of survival of the fittest, they are at least representative of the not unfit. They are smart, workmanlike horses. It is absolutely necessary that a regiment should be as sound in its horseflesh as in its men. Theoretically no remounts are accepted that are not looked over on level ground, on a road, or in a large yard, for it is easy to pass a bad horse in a field, or on a hillside, or in deep pasture, or when under cover, or in a drove. It is not safe to choose an underbred animal, immediately conspicuous by his coarse head, or thick throat, or short neck, or large, bony joints, or clumsy legs, or short pasterns, or curly in the hair of his mane or tail. The typical cavalry horse must have a small lean head, a flat, broad forehead, fine, full nostrils, a good, clean throat, thin neck, well-shaped legs, long pasterns, and straight hair, with a deep, wide chest, and short, broad back and loin. No long backs will do, for long backs do not carry weight, and short necks or croups are simply impossible for soldiering. Of course the horse has to be of the regimental colour. In the cavalry generally chestnuts are not in favour, for chestnuts usually have white, and white, except in the Scots Greys, is not desirable; neither chestnuts then, nor mealy bays, are fit for cavalry work, but roans and bays and browns, and for our Guardsmen blacks.

These are bought when rising four years old, and require about six months' training by the rough riders before they can be passed out of the riding school as efficient by the colonel. The Knightsbridge riding school is about forty-five yards long by sixteen wide, and in it perhaps fourteen young horses at a time will be at work, though the number of course depends on what the horses have to do. Their training is not as simple as might at first appear. The soldier has only one hand to work his horse with, and what an ordinary rider would do with the other hand he has to do with his leg. How skilfully he manages to guide by leg pressure is known to those who have seen the Musical Ride at the annual Military Tournament, which is little more than the ordinary practice of the riding school. But it should not be forgotten that the horse has to be taught to understand this pressure, and that his training is almost as long a business as that of his rider.

Very early in the morning, so as not to alarm the passers-by, the young horse is taught to stand fire by having a gun discharged close to him, and being encouraged to smell the powder and the smoking weapon ; he thus becomes familiar with the sound and scent, much as a boy does, though there is nothing to show that he ever associates the idea of being shot with the report which he soon treats with indifference. When once he is trained his work becomes lighter, and he cannot be said to have a hard life in London, an occasional outing at Wimbledon being his severest trial. Being condemned at fourteen, his full service is a little over ten years; but it is rare that he reaches the limit, and his average military life is between six and seven. When it is over he goes back to the depôt, and thence he often comes again by way of the sale yard into the London crowd.

CHAPTER XIII

THE SALE YARD

THE number of horses in London used exclusively for riding is very small. Taking them altogether, and including the police and military with the rest of the community, we shall not have one per cent. of the general herd. A good many of these are introduced direct from the dealers, but a large number are knocked in, and down, at Tattersall's.

Tattersall's is usually looked upon as the headquarters of horsey London. It is certainly the headquarters of the horse of pleasure, but, as has been made clear enough in these pages, that sort of horse is simply lost in the thousands that throng our streets. Tattersall's is practically the great betting exchange, but the visitor to any of the Monday or Thursday sales will be puzzled to find the least sign of a betting atmosphere at Knightsbridge. The two things are as distinct on those days as, say, the Bank of England and Capel Court. The yard is under cover, a lofty glass-roofed hall, which cost 30,000*l.* to build, and which is as big as many a railway station. It is surrounded by a handsome gallery, behind the arched and columned screen of which every type of pleasure vehicle seems to be 'on view,' duly

numbered in 'lots' for the hammer. In the centre of
the gravel area is a drinking fountain, surmounted by
the quaint old Georgian bust of the founder, with its
eyes fixed on the entrance doors, and its thoughts apparently as far away from water as are those of the
crowd around.

It is a different variety of crowd from that which
gathers in any other sale yard. London has several
'repositories.' There is Aldridge's in St. Martin's
Lane; there is Rymill's in the Barbican—these two
being the chief; and there are Stapleton's out in the
East, and Ward's in the West, and the Elephant and
Castle in the South, and others which many a horse
knows well. There is a sort of horse that 'knows the
lot'; the sort that 'does the round,' and brings more
money to the auctioneers than to the unfortunate
buyers, who 'find him out' in a fortnight, and 'get rid
of him sharp' to an unwary successor; a wonderful
animal this horse, 'quiet in harness, a good worker,'
who has only two faults, one that 'it takes a long time
to catch him in a field,' the other that 'he is not worth
a rap when caught.' But this kind of horse does not
put in many appearances at Knightsbridge. Tattersall's
has a character to keep up, and it has kept it up for
over a hundred years now. It is eminently respectable,
from the unused drinking fountain and the auctioneers'
hammer, one of the good old pattern, with a rounded
knob instead of a double head, down to the humblest
hanger-on.

Entering one of the stables which open on to the
yard, and have a dozen or more roomy stalls apiece, we
find a horse being measured, to make sure he is correctly

described. One would think he was a recruit, from the careful way in which the long wooden arm is brought down so gingerly as not even to press in his skin. Soon his turn will come. Up in the gallery will go his number, and the young auctioneer in the rostrum below —which has a sounding-board, as if it were a cathedral pulpit—will read out his short title.

Out comes the horse at last—tittuppy-trot, tittuppy-trot. 'Ten,' says one of the crowd. 'Ten guineas,' echoes the auctioneer. 'Twelve,' comes from the crowd; 'twelve guineas,' echoes the 'Varsity man in the pulpit. And so the game goes on with nods and shouts, each nod or look being worth a guinea, so that the solo runs, 'Thirteen—thirteen guineas—fourteen guineas—fifteen guineas—sixteen—sixteen guineas— seventeen—eighteen—twenty guineas'—quite a sing-song up to—'twenty-eight guineas'—and so gradually slowing, with a spurt or two to 'forty guineas'—and then a grand noisy rally till 'fifty-five' is reached. 'Fifty-five ?—Fifty-five ?—Fifty-five ? Last time, Fifty-five!'—knock—and away goes Captain Carbine's hunter, to make room for a 'match pair' that will change hands at 165 guineas, or perhaps fifty more if the season has begun—the bidding always in guineas, in order that the auctioneer may live on the shillings, as Sir John Gilbert used to do in the old days when the guineas flowed to him for his drawings on the wood.

If you want riding horses or carriage horses you go to Tattersall's ; if you want draught horses for trade, you go to Rymill's or Aldridge's, where you not only get the new-comers, but also the second-hand, and many-another-hand, from London's stables.   With those second-hand horses we need not overburden ourselves ; our task has been to bring the first-hand horses into London, and sort them out.   We have brought in the 'bus horses, the tram horses, the cab horses, the railway horses, the cart and many other horses.   Of the cart horses we could, if it were worth while, say a good deal more.   We have said nothing of the distillers, the millers, the soap merchants, the timber merchants, the better class contractors, and half a dozen other first-hand horse-owning trades.   Some of the distillers' horses are said, by those who know, to be as good as any in the brewers' drays, and by ' as good ' is meant that they are of the same breeding, and can be compared with them, owing to their being at somewhat similar work.

If you think you know anything of horseflesh and want the conceit taken out of you, by all means attend a repository sale.   You will see a horse—it may be a likely mare—led from her stall and stood ready for her turn, and you will probably value her at, to be reasonable, 20*l.* ; and she looks worth not a penny less. When her number goes up at the window you will see her shown at her best at a run, and, for a moment, you will be inclined to add 5*l.* to your estimate.   But soon a chill will run down your back as you hear the bidding. ' Three !   Three and a half !   Four ! ' a long pause. ' Four and a half !   Five ! ' jerks the auctioneer in the corner, with about as much expression as if a penny had been put in his mouth to work him automatically. ' For the last time !   Five ! '   Knock.   Five guineas ! And as the mare is led back to her stall she seems to change before your very eyes, and you are ready to admit that she doesn't look worth a penny more !

There is rather a good story of grey—or chestnut ? —age, told of, or probably shaped to fit, one of these repositories where horses are knocked down at the rate of thirty lots an hour. A certain colonel happened to peep in during a sale, and saw a smart-looking cob being shown amid a dead silence on the part of the shabby-looking crowd. ' What do you bid, gentlemen ? ' asked the auctioneer. ' Two ! ' said the colonel sportively. There was no advance ; and to the colonel's astonishment, the lot was knocked down to him. He handed the clerk a five-pound note in payment. ' Really, sir, I'm sorry I must send for change,' said the clerk. ' Oh, never mind,' said the colonel, ' I'll take it out in horses ! '

The man who says he knows everything about horses—and he is rather a common object of the street —seems to compare all horses he sees with a thoroughbred racer, and knocks them off as beauties or beasts in the terms of that comparison. He forgets, or does not know, that there are other stud-books than those that come from Weatherby's, and that the different breeds of horse are made and kept alive for their fitness for different occupations; and he also forgets, or never knew, that there is no man living competent to judge all down the lines that lead and mingle from the pedigree stallions of the Racing, Cleveland, Clydesdale, Shire, Suffolk, Pony, Hackney, and other stud-books.

As regards what we may call the ' medium ' brigade, the lighter cart horses, or vanners, of no particular class or pedigree, the opinion of the man in the street, though valueless, is not unreasonable. They are, it must be confessed, a curiously miscellaneous lot, most of them not doing half enough work for their weight, owing to their power being at the wrong end. They come early on the scene, some of them at four years old, and they linger late. For the first year or two they fetch from forty to sixty guineas, seldom more, and they sort themselves out rapidly into the twenty-pound line, owing to their being unequal to the work that is put behind them. ' Call that a horse! ' we heard recently from the depths of the crowd in the Poultry. ' Why, he has got no power astern ; he climbs along ! ' And that is exactly the state of the case with hundreds of the London vanners. But then such horses are possible because they are cheap, and we must not expect too much of them. Their life is a hard one. As a rule, they are worked long and wearily ; but, un-like ' that useful horse, the hackney,' they have a Sunday's rest.

This rest on the seventh day is far more important to a horse's well-being than many a hackney owner is disposed to admit. Burke, in a letter to a member of the National Assembly of France, in 1794, attributed much of the evil of the Reign of Terror to the con-tinuance of sittings without the intermission of the Day of Rest. ' They who always labour,' he said, ' can have no clear judgment. You never give yourselves time to cool, and exhaust your brains like men who burn out their candles and are left in the dark.' Wilberforce used to warn Pitt that he would shorten his life if he worked without rest. Mr. Gladstone ascribes much of his vigorous old age to his Sabbath rest. Apart from the religious view of the question, it is notable that even in Paris the desire for a day of rest is more and more increasing. A meeting was lately held there, in the hall of the Geographical Society, by an association called ' The People's League for Sunday Rest.' Churchmen and laymen, Protestants and Roman Catholics, and all classes were represented, the Abbé Garnier closing with an eloquent address on the advantages to the State of a periodical respite from toil.

And necessary as it may be for man, it is at least as necessary for his horse. In the famous speech of Lord Erskine, on introducing for the first time in the House of Peers a bill dealing with cruelty to animals, he spoke much about the ' rights ' of those over whom we have been given the mastery. ' Man's dominion,' he said, ' over the lower animals is very large ; and it is his not merely by superior knowledge and power, but also by Divine appointment. The dominion is not absolute, but is limited by the obligations of justice and mercy ' —as declared in the Commandment, where the cattle are in this respect placed on the same footing as the children, the servants, and the stranger within the gates. The mercy of which injunction is manifest, even were its wisdom not one of the commonplaces of experience.

A most gratifying testimony to the soundness of this ancient law, even—to use his own words—' as a mere matter of business,' was given by Bianconi at an early meeting of the British Association for the Advancement of Science. Before the railroad found its way to Ireland, the whole of the mail traffic was there run on Bianconi's cars. He thus came to own more horses than any man of his time, and he averred that as the result of many years' trial he got far more work out of them when he ran them for only six days a week, and that for a long period he had made it a rule to give each of them a weekly day of rest.

'A merciful man is merciful to his beast,' or, in Scriptural phrase, 'A righteous man regardeth the life of his beast; but the tender mercies of the wicked are cruel.'[1] If Justice requires that the rights of animals should be considered, much more does Mercy extend to their treatment. 'There is implanted by Nature,' says Lord Bacon, 'in the heart of man, a noble and excellent affection of mercy extending even to the brute animals, which by Divine appointment are subjected to this dominion.' Dr. Chalmers, in his eloquent sermon on Humanity to Animals, amplified and emphasised this. 'It is,' he said, 'a virtue which oversteps as it were the limits of a species, and which prompts a descending movement on our part, of righteousness and mercy towards those who have an inferior place to ourselves in the scale of creation. It is not the circulation of benevolence within the limits of one species. It is the transmission of it from one species to another. The first is the charity of a world. The second is the charity of a universe. Had there been no such charity, no descending current of love and of compassion from species to species, what, I ask, would have become of ourselves? . . . The distance upward between us and that mysterious Being who let Himself down from heaven's high concave upon our lowly platform, surpasses by infinity the distance downward between us

[1] Proverbs xii. 10.

and everything that breathes. And He bowed Himself thus far for the purpose of an example, as well as for the purpose of an expiation, that every Christian might extend his compassionate regards over the whole of sentient and suffering Nature.' By Dr. Chalmers the duty of mercy to animals was thus lifted to the highest level of Christian ethics. In the same spirit are the words of that distinguished man of science and philanthropist, Dr. George Wilson :—' There is an example as well as a lesson for us in the Saviour's compassion for men. Inasmuch as we partake with the lower animals of bodies exquisitely sensitive to pain, and often agonised by it, we should be slow to torture creatures who, though not sharers of our joys, or participators in our mental agonies, can equal us in bodily suffering. We stand, by Divine appointment, between God and His irresponsible subjects, and are as gods to them.'

Descending from this high level of moral and religious duty, it may be remarked that absolute cruelty to horses is much on the decrease, owing chiefly to the activity of the police. But a growing proportion of horses of a certain class have their lives shortened and their value rapidly deteriorated by persistent overwork. Many of them, as Sir Benjamin Richardson says, 'go from early life to premature death without the attention a steam-engine receives'—the learned doctor being evidently aware that even a steam-engine has to be treated as daintily as a baby if it is to last long and work well—and the worst used of all our horses are the weary nags in traps and spring carts that crawl home so late on Sunday nights. In short, the hackney is too useful a horse for his own good. Six days a week he works to earn money, and on the seventh he works to spend it. And so he is soon knocked up, and changes hands oftener than any horse in London.

Yet one more class of first-handers, and that is the ponies, which keep to their first owners longer, and, in the ownership of sweeps, attain frequently quite a remarkable healthy old age. And with the first-hand ponies and hackneys our herd reaches the 150,000, and we confirm the usual estimate that half the London horses are at least second-hand.

Three hundred thousand horses! Not a tenth of what there are in this island; but what a herd it seems! And what are they worth? Taking them at 25*l.* apiece they would run to 7,500,000*l.*, and that, as we have seen, would be putting them at a low price. To keep them at less than half a sovereign a week we should require seven and a half millions a year; and if we add to this current cost the interest on the capital sunk in them, and their harness, the wages paid in looking after them, and the rent of their stables, we shall get into figures that seem almost too large to be true.

CHAPTER XIV

THE DONKEY MART

THE London donkey exchange is the Islington Cattle Market on a Friday afternoon. There some 3,000 'mokes' change hands during a year, the busiest days being the Fridays before and after Bank Holidays, for on these festive occasions there are not a few 'donkeys of pleasure' which remain in the same ownership for just seven days, and in that time pay the cost of their purchase and keep and bring the profit on their re-sale.

The biggest of the batches paying toll at Islington come from Ireland. Sometimes a herd of a hundred, sometimes even more, will be met with on the road from Milford or Holyhead, steadily journeying towards the city to which so many hoofs point, and feeding by the wayside as they come ; or, and this is the more usual method, crowded in truck-loads on the rail. Not that these big herds are thrown on the market all at once, for the donkey dealer knows his business, and rarely puts in an appearance at Islington with more than a score ; the trade is a trade of ones, and twos, and threes, which change owners with much arguing and bargaining, and in which nearly every argument and abatement is emphasised with a more or less affectionate

THE PICK OF THE MARKET

whack on the unfortunate animal's back. The stick-play at a donkey sale is remarkable. 'Sure, sir,' said one of the bystanders, 'the Neddies feel themselves quite at home!'

The track, on the high road, of an Irish donkey drove is easily recognisable owing to the heavy shoes it is the custom to wear in the Emerald Isle—shoes which are promptly replaced by the lighter English pattern as

WAITING THEIR TURN

soon as the purchase goes to his new home. Irish are not, however, the heaviest shoes; for those we must go to Egypt, where the native farriers simply cover the feet with a plate. Shoeing a donkey costs sixpence a foot, and the farrier does not 'hanker after it.' 'You see, sir,' we heard one of them say, 'it's not nearly so easy as a horse; it is a smaller shoe and finer work, and some of the brutes have to be lashed up, and some put on their backs with their feet in the air. However, two shillings is the price for a set, and we cannot raise it, and there's an end of it! Luckily, the shoes last a couple of months!'

We have been assured by a donkey expert that the Irishmen always bray with a brogue, and that without this they would often be unrecognisable; but recent experience has taught us to our sorrow that humorists of the libellous kind are not unknown among donkey drivers. Perhaps our driver had an unusually cultivated ear for vocal music; any way, after a day's drill we have not found it difficult to identify an Irish donkey nine times out of ten.

There are over 200,000 donkeys in Ireland employed in agriculture, and these are of all sizes, some of the larger having a strain of horse blood in them, as is the case in Italy, where the so-called donkey is a by no means insignificant animal. Italy has more donkeys than any other European country, there being over 700,000 of them there; while France, which of late years has taken to that most difficult of pursuits, mule breeding, has 400,000. The great mule-breeding country is, however, the United States, where there are two and a half millions of mules and donkeys taken together, it being found impossible to separate them owing to the varying proportions of horse ancestry producing an indefinite series from the genuine mule to the asinine mulatto. For the male mule is not always sterile, and the female will breed with horse or ass, or apparently any species of equus.

Next on the list to Ireland, as a source of supply to the London Donkey Market, is 'gallant little Wales,' whose natives also are credited with a note of their own, shrill, persistent, and distressing, though welcome in the owner's ear, for a Welsh donkey is generally a good one; in fact, Wales breeds our best donkeys, and some of them will even fetch as much as 30*l*.

Donkey breeding has its difficulties, and it does not pay in England. Now that the commons have been inclosed, or taken over by County Councils, and the common rights done away with, pasture for nothing is rarely obtainable, and the margin of profit on a donkey is too small to be worth troubling about. Prices are ' up ' now, it is true, and a donkey that a few years ago could be had for eighteen shillings will now be cheap at fifty, but the ordinary work-a-day animal does not range much above that price, which we can take as a fair average market rate.

The market has not a thriving look about it. The great area at Islington, with its labyrinth of rails and posts, is all bare except in one corner, and in that about three of the roads are filled, one with donkeys, one with a series of scattered marine stores of harness and horsey sundries, and one with the most miserably weedy ponies and drudges that ever greet the horse-buyer's eye. Here is the tail end of London's horse-world, the last refuge of our cheapest beasts of burden, the last chance of the pony, and the first chance of the donkey, brought together so as to show off the donkey to advantage. Great is the clatter as the weedy nags, all heads and legs, are bustled about over the stones, with a whip here and a whip there to make them swerve and scamper as they are shown off before the ' nibbler.' ' We call 'em nibblers, sir, 'cos they don't always bite ! ' There is a

ON SALE

refreshing candour about the whole affair which effec-
tually disarms criticism. ' He ain't much to look at,
mister, but then I don't ask much. He might suit you
at the price. Four pun ten ain't much for a oss !'

'Try a donkey, sir?' Well, one would rather.
A good donkey is a better servant than a bad horse.
In proportion to his size he will bear a heavier burden
and drag a greater weight. He will eat not a quarter
of what a horse does, and he will live at least twice as
long. ' How long will a donkey live?' we asked Mr.
Gill of Hampstead. ' Live? Well, I know one that has
lived thirty-seven years and seen three generations of
the family from babhood to babhood!'

And what becomes of the dead donkeys? A good
many go in their last days to this Mr. Gill, who supplies
them wholesale to the Veterinary College for dissecting
purposes, the anatomy of the donkey being almost
identical with that of the horse—in fact, a donkey is
practically a horse, minus the callosities on the hind
legs, and plus the tufted tail and long ears.

The dead or moribund horse goes to the knackers,
' the practical zootomists,' as they are beginning to
call themselves, but the knacker will rarely have
anything to do with the donkey, which is hardly worth
the cost of carriage. Five shillings is his outside value
for his hoofs, his bones, and skin—chiefly his skin, out
of which we get shagreen leather and memorandum
tablets, and perhaps a drumhead or two, though drum-
heads are nowadays mostly made of Canadian deerskin.
The flesh is worthless. It is only the Persian who will
eat ass's flesh, and even he must have it wild, after
hunting it, as if asses were deer.

Most of these Islington donkeys would require little hunting. But why this abrupt return to donkeys? Why not asses? The reason is that though ass is the more scientific—and Semitic—it is the more unpopular, owing apparently to the old Egyptians, who originated the libel of the animal's stupidity, and to the Mediævalists, who made him the symbol of St. Thomas. With us he is the great ass, for English is the only language in which the old word does not appear as a diminutive; even in Latin he is *as-inus*, and in German he is *es-el*. Ass sounds so very exclusive amongst us, while there is something pleasant and companionable about donkey, for a double diminutive always shows appreciation. No unlovable hoiden was ever called a 'lassiekie'; and donkey—dun, dunnie, dunniekie—is built on similar lines. 'Oh, you dear little, wee little donkey!' we overheard on Hampstead Heath; a phrase which an etymologist would render as, 'Oh, you dear little, little, little, little, little ass!' And some of these London donkeys are very little, though they are not so small as those in the ownership of low-caste Hindoos; and they would look mere dwarfs by the side of the big Spanish donkeys used by the Marquis of Salisbury in his Hatfield hay-carts, which must stand at least thirteen hands. But then the donkeys of Spain and Calabria will often run into more, and one of their stallions will fetch 200*l.* when bought for export to Kentucky for mule breeding, and also donkey breeding; the animal known as 'donkey' there being now as big as any in the world, and ranging from fourteen to fifteen hands. And even by the banks of the Ohio the donkey betrays his origin by his hereditary aversion to cross running water, and his delight in rolling in the dust, as his ancestors delighted to roll in their arid desert home.

The donkey of our streets is a better animal than he used to be. He is bigger and healthier, he is fed better, and he does more work. The work done by these donkeys is remarkable; I have known one in the shafts of a South London milk-cart which for eight months travelled 140 miles a week in doing the daily round.

Some of this improvement is certainly due to the shows, the chief of which is the triennial one, which now sometimes holds its meeting at the People's Palace. A queer show is this, for not only do the donkeys come, but they have to bring with them their barrows all duly loaded up with vegetables, or fish, or firewood, or whatever it may be, out of which the ' commercial traveller,' as the costermonger now calls himself, earns his living. Of course every donkey has a name, such a name as one would give to a horse—many of the names such as are borne by winning race-horses. Some of the donkeys have been working for their owners seven, ten, or fifteen years; some of them are even entered as twenty years old; and in most cases, without a rest, they have worked their six days a week, year in, year out. Every donkey has his price, often as fictitious as that given at a bird show, but occasionally genuine and such as would lead to business, even though it may be 15*l*. or 20*l*. or 30*l*. Even at Islington these high-priced animals are to be met with, but not in the pens; they are in the light carts and barrows of the donkey dealers, who would think it *infra dig.* to drive a pony. Some of these thoroughbreds have pedigrees going back for several generations, and the starting of a Donkey Stud Book is evidently an event of the near future.

Away from the crowd, in a pen by themselves, harnessed up to their traps and with cloths over them, we find two of these aristocrats admirably groomed and in the pink of condition. The cloth is taken off one that we may inspect her. 'That is White Jenny. She'll do her six miles inside thirty minutes any day you please!' 'And the other?' 'The Skewbald? He is as good.' 'And what is Jenny worth?' 'Forty-five pounds, not a penny less!' 'But is that not rather a long price?' 'Maybe, but she's good. What is a good horse worth compared to a bad one? How do you know a good horse from a bad one? By opinion. And that is how we know a good donkey from a bad one. That is not the highest price asked for a donkey. Why, I know a pair that changed hands for a hundred and twenty pounds—yes, one hundred and twenty; sixty pounds apiece!'

And yet such scope is there for opinion that the rates at which the lots are being parted for in the market do not average as many shillings. This is for 'Jacks' for ordinary driving among costers and organmen. But we are here reminded that there is a curious by-way of the donkey world concerning itself with 'milch asses.' These have been bought for 12*l.*, but they generally range from 7*l.* to 8*l.*, being sold again after six months at from 2*l.* to 3*l.* Asses' milk was at one time a favourite with physicians. Being more sugary and less cheesy than that of the cow, it was well suited for weaklings and invalids of a consumptive turn, and a fairly large business was done in it. But the patent foods came in with their voluminous advertisements, and the trade has almost died out. It is most in evidence in one or two of the West End squares during the season, where a donkey, with a goat in the cart, may be seen in the morning going round to be milked. If there are fifty milch asses in London it is as much as there are, the oldest firm at work being that of Dawkins, of Bolsover Street, which has been selling asses' milk ever since 1780, and, what is more extraordinary, jobbing out milch asses to families, sending them far and wide into the country, accompanied with full printed directions as to how to milk and treat them. As an ass will yield about a quart a day, the London supply could easily be got into a single churn, and is manifestly microscopic, but the jobbing is not so insignificant a business, and is certainly worth a note.

Donkey jobbing in its draught and riding branches exists, but does not flourish. Here and there one hears of men with studs ranging up to fifty, but they are not numerous. Ten is the average stud of the donkey master, and there are about five hundred donkeys thus ' standing at livery.' It is not a satisfactory business to run, and many people have burnt their fingers at it. A donkey out on hire for a month is at the mercy of his hirer, who is not always merciful, and it is frequently returned so over-driven and knocked about that it takes two months to return to decent condition ; and as the charge for hire is three shillings a week, the twelve shillings spread over three months is not much to get a living out of, although it may mean 75 per cent. per annum on the capital invested. The poor willingly pay high percentages, owing to the amounts they deal with being so trifling. The same rule holds good in all trades; on a large return a living is possible on a small percentage, but where the return is small the percentage must be large. No wonder, then, that to hire a donkey many a costermonger has to borrow the money at 20 per cent. per week.

Many of the donkeys at the Islington market appear there two or three times during the year, and all the 3,000 are not used up in London, for Brighton and Margate and other seaside pleasure towns are supplied from the London centre. Against this we must put the private sales, for many of our donkeys change hands without visiting Islington. Altogether there seem to be about thirteen thousand donkeys in the county of London. These mostly begin work at two years old, though they ought not to begin until they are four, and they are very seldom used for riding purposes until they have turned three.

But the riding donkeys are few in number. On recent application to the County Council, we were officially informed that only fifty-seven drivers now hold licences to let out donkeys on the open spaces under the Council's control, and that each licence only entitles the holder to let out five animals.

There is at present no special breed for riding, the donkey being in the same state as the horse, whose shape and make decide whether the mount or the draught is to be his line in life ; and the best begin with ' pleasure,' and take to ' business ' in the shafts later on.

About twelve years would seem to be the average London life, most of the veterans being disposed of at last for country work. A donkey seldom breaks down. He is one of the healthiest of animals, and one of the cheapest to feed. He is so clean and careful that he rarely troubles the vet. He will not drink greasy or dirty water ; he would rather go without and die of thirst. His food must be fresh ; no leavings will suit him. Once a donkey has breathed over fodder in a nose-bag no other donkey will touch it, nor will he touch food that has been breathed over by any other animal. Like the knight, he must have an egg to himself, although, like the gallant Schweppermann, he will not object to two. One good meal a day of, perhaps, chaff and oats, and beans and hay, with some pudding or bread from his master's table, is his usual fare ; but he only has corn when he is at work, and his hay is often that newly mown from a gentleman's lawn. He takes kindly to potatoes and carrots, but he objects to a Saturday ' mash.' He is very sound on his feet, and is rarely troubled by contagious diseases—in short, he is a sanitarian, and almost proof against epidemics.

He has very strict notions as to what constitutes a day's work, and once he gets home will never go out again that day if he can help it; and it requires immense persuasion, and no little force, to get him to work on a Sunday, for, like his humble master, he has a very strong objection to working more than six days a week. Some people tell us that the greyer he is the stupider he is, but it appears on investigation that those who hold the opinion have generalised on a very few examples, as is the way of the world in most

ON RETURN

other matters. He is said always to bear the ' ancestral stripe,' but this is gradually being bred out of him.

Those who would see the coster's donkey at his best should go to Billingsgate or the vegetable markets early in the morning. There they will find him smartened up by his drive from home, and contentedly waiting for his load; and they will probably be astonished at his being on the whole so cheery and well. Donkeys on hire are often ill-treated, but a donkey driven by his owner is generally looked after kindly, inasmuch as few men care to damage their own property. Many of these costers' donkeys come pattering along with a briskness and assurance that can only come of contentment with their work, and some of the smallest even are as active and ' packed with power ' as one could wish, and with a quiet, fearless outlook, speaking volumes for their master. Here and there some exceptionally good-looking examples will be pointed out to a new-comer as ' known in the shows ' or ' on the road,' and hoping to be better known, perhaps next year in the Donkey Derby which is being organised by Mr. John Atkinson, the well-known medical superintendent of the Animals' Institute in Wilton Place ; the idea of the competition being that racing will improve the breed by encouraging emulation among the breeders.

At the same time the donkey is hardly a racer at present, although donkey-racing is not unknown, and that under two very different forms. There is the ' comic ' style, usually indulged in at country fairs and travelling circuses, in which the rider's object is to reach the winning-post last, owing to the prize being given to the hindmost; and there is the more straight-forward, but certainly less exciting, variety, in which the first past the judge is the winner. If we could have a race of this kind, in which the skill of the rider were rewarded in inverse ratio to his use of the stick, such a competition would not fail of support : but that it will not do to forbid the use of the stick altogether was shown some years ago at the Agricultural Hall, where, as a conclusion to the show, a race took place in which no sticks were allowed, and the result was such a display of tugging at mouths and kicking at ribs on the part of the riders, and poking and prodding with sticks and umbrellas on the part of the crowd, that the least said about it the better.

And this Derby reminds us of another, which, however, was a man who spelt his name with an ' *a.*' He was a fish-salter who was driving home from Billingsgate one morning when his donkey caught his foot in a plug-hole and broke it between the knee and the fetlock. What was to be done ? ' Kill him ! ' said the crowd. ' No ! ' said Darby. ' I'll not kill him ; I'll cure him ! ' and putting him on the cart, he dragged him home. He put the patient to bed in his own sitting-room, bandaged him, looked after him, and had him on the high road to recovery, when Mrs. Darby, who happened to be a washerwoman at the London Hospital, let out the secret of the queer patient, and awoke an interest in the matter which led to a country home being offered to the interesting convalescent as soon as he was able to travel. And eighteen months after the leg was broken Darby drove up in triumph to Billingsgate with his pet ' as sound as ever.'

This is, of course, an exceptional instance. Costers' donkeys are not generally tended in sitting-rooms, though their stable accommodation is peculiarly varied. A shed or a lean-to against the back-yard wall seems to be the prevailing fashion, with the cart alongside and the harness indoors; for the harness may be worth as much as the cart or the donkey. A good set will cost 7*l.*, a bad one may be had for as many pence, there being a lower depth in rag and rope than that displayed in the marine stores on the Islington stones, where the line seems to be drawn at the old carriage harness, which makes the poor little donkey look like a street Arab in a man's coat.

Miserable as many of these turn-outs may look—animal, harness, and vehicle complete—it will be found that they ' bulk into money.' There are 7,500*l.* worth of donkeys alone changing hands at the London mart during the year, and the carts are worth quite as much as the power that draws them. The costermonger begins business with a basket; from that he advances to a hand-truck; and from that, when he has amassed sufficient capital, he rises to the dignity of the donkey-cart, which made its first appearance amongst us in the days of Elizabeth, when donkeys first became common in these islands.

Previous to then the few donkeys we had were, it would seem, used for riding purposes only, as the high-class Syrian breed is used to-day. Those who would see donkeys at their best, to Syria must go. In that interesting land they have become differentiated into four distinct breeds: the rough one, for ordinary draught; the heavy one, used for agriculture; the

Arab one, used for ordinary riding; and the light and graceful one, reserved as a mount for ladies only, which only very distantly resembles the patient variety on which the London mater-familias of sixteen stone enjoys a few anxious minutes on high days and holidays.

It may seem a mystery why the donkey market should be held in such an unexpected place. Of course, it went there from Smithfield with the cattle market. But why did it begin at Smithfield? For the same reason as the cattle market did; because the animals could be conveniently watered at the old Horse Pool, which once lay between the moor fields and the smooth field that served the citizens as a playground. And the Friday market on that field was at least as old as the days of Fitzstephen, and even in those days it included the draught animals and 'peasants' wares' we find represented to-day among the posts and rails of Islington.

CHAPTER XV

THE END

VERY few horses are allowed to end their days in peace, after long and faithful service, like the Duke of Wellington's old charger Copenhagen, in the paddocks at Strathfieldsaye. London horses, in particular, rarely die natural deaths. Many of them are sent back into the country in a vain hope that they will 'come round'; many of them are poleaxed for very shame at their miserable appearance; some of them slip and injure themselves beyond recovery in the streets.

A dreadful object this of a suffering horse, sprawling in one of our main roads with the usual crowd around it. 'Why cannot he be killed at once? Why must he linger in agony? Surely——' Quite so, gentle reader, and indignant letter-writer to the daily newspapers, but do not be in a hurry! The driver has no right to order the horse to be killed; it is not his property, but his master's; and before he can give the order the master has to be found, and the master does not, in many cases, care to lose his horse irrevocably, and appeals to his vet.; and so, while the driver is finding his master, and the master is finding his vet., the horse lies suffering in the street. When the needful

permission is obtained, a telephone message to Harrison
Barber brings the cart on the scene, and within half an
hour of that message the horse is not only dead, but
being cut up in one of the Harrison Barber depôts.
There are seven of these depôts in strategical positions
round and in London, where the carts are kept cleaned
and in readiness, tools and all, like fire engines, ready
to be turned out and on the way in less than five
minutes from the receipt of the call.

A curious trade is that of the horse-slaughterer,
who must not only have a licence, but carry on his
operations in accordance with the 26th of George III.
and other Acts of Parliament. No horse that enters his
yard must come out again alive, or as a horse. The
moment it enters those gates it must be disfigured by
having its mane cut off so close to the skin as to spoil
its value, and though it may be put in a ' pound ' on
the premises, which might better be called a condemned
cell or a moribundary, it must not remain there for more
than three days.

In Garratt Lane, Wandsworth, is the largest horse-
slaughtering yard in London. It has existed for about
a hundred years. There it stands, practically odour-
less, by the banks of the winding Wandle, with a wide
meadow in front of it and a firework factory next door,
the magazine of which is within measurable distance
of its boiler-house. One fine morning—it was really a
beautiful morning—we found our way down the lane,
along the field, armed with Mr. Ross's permit, to be
initiated by Mr. Milestone into the mysteries of a
horse's departure from the London world.

The last scene does not take long. In two seconds

a horse is killed; in a little over half an hour his hide is in a heap of dozens, his feet are in another heap, his bones are boiling for oil, his flesh is cooking for cat's meat. Maneless he stands; a shade is put over his eyes; a swing of the axe, and, with just one tremor, he falls heavy and dead on the flags of a spacious kitchen, which has a line of coppers and boilers steaming against two of its walls.

In a few minutes his feet are hooked up to cross-beams above, and two men pounce upon him to flay him; for the sooner he is ready the quicker he cooks. Slash, slash, go the knives, and the hide is peeled off about as easily as a tablecloth; and so clean and un-injured is the body that it looks like the muscle model we see in the books and in the plaster casts at the corn-chandler's. Then, with full knowledge gained by almost life-long practice, for the trade is hereditary, the meat is slit off with razor-like knives, and the bones are left white and clean and yet unscraped, even the neck vertebræ being cleared in a few strokes—one of the quickest things in carving imaginable.

If there is any malformation the sweep of the knife is stayed for a moment; that is all. The same sort of thing has always been seen before, and there is no hesi-tation about the way to deal with it. No matter of what breed or age or condition the horse may be, his ' boning ' is not delayed by peculiarities. And horses of all sorts, some of them sound and in the prime of life, here meet their doom—the favourite horse killed at his master's death, to save him from falling into cruel hands: the runaway horse that has injured a daughter; the brute that has begun to kick and bite; the mildest-mannered mare that has, perhaps, merely taken a wrong turn and made her mistress angry—all come here to die with the hundreds of the injured and the old. Taking them all round, the old and young and sound and ailing, they average out in the men's opinion at rather over eleven years when they here meet their doom.

Soon the bare skeleton remains to be broken up, and in baskets go aloft to be shot into a huge digester, where it is made to yield about a quarter hundred-weight of oil. Following the oil, we see it cleared of its stearin, pressed out between huge sheets of paper, and remaining in white cakes like gauffres ready for the candle-makers; and we see the oil flowing limpid and clear into the tank above, from which it is barrelled off to be used eventually for lubricating and leather-dressing purposes.

Returning to the bones, we find them out on the flags, clean and free from grease, ready to be thrown into a mill, from which they emerge like granite from a stonebreaker, along a sloping cylindrical screen, which sorts the fragments into sizes varying up to half an inch. And stretching away from us are sacks, full to the brim with bones, all in rows like flour-sacks at a miller's, all ready to go off to the manure merchants. And still further following the bones, we find some of them ground to powder and mixed with sulphuric acid to leave the premises as another form of ferti-liser.

Having seen the bones off the premises, we follow the feet, of which we find a huge pile, not a trace of which will be left before the day is out. The skin and hoofs will go to the glue-makers and blue-makers; the bones will go to the button-makers; the old shoes will go to the farrier's and be used over and over again, welded in the fire and hammered on the streets, so that all that is lost of a horseshoe is what rusts or is rubbed off in powder.

With a glance at the tails and manes, which will soon be lost in sofas, chairs, or fishing-lines, we reach the heap of hides, which will probably find its way to Germany to be made into the leather guards on cavalry trousers, or, maybe, stay in this country for carriage roofs and whip-lashes. This distribution of the dead horse may seem to be an odoriferous business, but the odours are reduced to a minimum by an elaborate ventilating system which draws off all the fumes and emanations into a line of pipes, and passes them over a wide furnace to be burnt, so that none of them reach the outer air.

But now for the 'meat,' which, cut into such joints as the trade require, has been boiling in the coppers and is now done to a turn, with just the central tint of redness and rawness that suits the harmless, necessary cat, while the 'tripe' is doing white in another copper to suit the palate of the less fastidious dog.

Harrison Barber, Limited, the successors of the once great Jack Atcheler, dead some thirty years since, kill 26,000 London horses a year. All night and all day the work goes on, this slaying and flaying, and boning and boiling down, and this cooking for feline food. Go to any of their depôts between five and six o'clock in the morning, and you will find a long string of the pony traps and hand-carts, barrows and perambulators,

THE LAST OF THE LONDON HORSE

used in the wholesale and retail cat's-meat trade. The
horse on an average yields 2 cwt. 3 qrs. of meat;
26,000 horses a year means 500 a week, which in its
turn means 70 tons of meat per week to feed the dogs
and cats of London.

This is not all the 'meat' that is sold, nor all the
London horses that are killed, for the horseflesh trade
is large enough to employ thirty wholesale salesmen;
but taking even this ten tons a day, we shall find it
means 134,400 meals, inasmuch as a pound of meat
cuts up into half a dozen ha'porths—the skewers being
given in, though it takes half a ton of them to fix up
a day's consumption. Here is another item for the
forest conservation people! $182\frac{1}{2}$ tons of deal used a
year in skewering up the horses made into meat by
Harrison Barber!

Sometimes there is a glut of the aged and the
maimed, and the supply of meat exceeds the demand.
To cope with this difficulty a complete refrigerating
plant is at work at Wandsworth, cooling the larders, in
which two hundred and fifty horses can be stored;
which larders are not only a revelation, but a welcome
surprise.

A door is opened and shut, and we stand in the
darkness between two doors in an air lock; the inner
door is opened and a shiver of cold runs through us as a
match is struck and a candle lighted; and there in
front is what looks like a deep cave in an arctic drift.
Around us are piles of meat, all hard as stone and
glittering with ice crystals; overhead, and at the back

of all, the beams and walls are thick with pure cling-
ing snow; and from above a few flakes fall as the door
closes on the silvery cloak that wraps the last to leave
the Horse World of London.

THE END